GBBHunter

AN INTRODUCTION
TO LOGIC

PHILOSOPHY

Editor
PROFESSOR H. J. PATON
M.A., F.B.A., D.LITT., LL.D.

*Emeritus Professor of Moral Philosophy
in the University of Oxford*

AN INTRODUCTION
TO LOGIC

DAVID MITCHELL

Fellow of Worcester College, Oxford
and University Lecturer in Philosophy

HUTCHINSON UNIVERSITY LIBRARY

LONDON

HUTCHINSON & CO. (*Publishers*) LTD
178-202 Great Portland Street, London W.1

London Melbourne Sydney
Auckland Bombay Toronto
Johannesburg New York

First published 1962

*This book has been set in Times New Roman. It has
been printed in Great Britain by William Clowes and
Sons Ltd, London and Beccles, and bound by them.*

CONTENTS

	Introduction	7
1	Logical form	9
2	The traditional logic of terms	24
3	The logic of propositions	47
4	Existence, predication and identity	73
5	Propositions and facts	101
6	Logic and language: I	120
7	Logic and language: II	136
8	Logical necessity	154
9	Generalisations and theories	167
	A short bibliography	189
	Index	190

INTRODUCTION

The purpose of this short book is to provide an elementary introduction to logical systems and to some of the central problems of
logical theory.

For the student of a hundred years ago elementary formal logic
consisted of the syllogistic logic of Aristotle, modified and added
to in the middle ages, but already for centuries stereotyped and
unchallenged. It provided material for exercises in the application
of rules learnt by heart, but it does not seem to have stimulated
thought or intellectual curiosity. But since then, and particularly in
the last sixty years, formal logic has come to life, and new systems of
logic, such as the calculus of propositions and the calculus of
predicates, have been devised. Whereas the exponents of traditional
logic were scholars trained in the literary and linguistic disciplines
of the Greek and Latin languages, the originators of modern logic
have been in the main mathematicians. We owe most of what is new
in logic to their investigations into the foundations of mathematics
and into the relations between logic and mathematical reasoning.

The revival of logic and the widening of its scope have not only
brought new discoveries but have also led to the critical re-examination of traditional doctrines. But, not surprisingly, the logical inno-
vators of our time have, like other pioneers, been more concerned
with breaking new ground than with establishing links between
their own discoveries and what went before. And since the notations
and manner of presentation of modern logical systems are very
different from those of the traditional logic, the relation between the
old and the new systems is not immediately apparent. Thus one of
the tasks which I have set myself is to show that the differences
between them are more apparent than real and that all may properly
be thought of as providing more or less complete and successful
analyses of the forms of valid argument. So, in brief surveys of the
traditional logic of terms (Chapter 2) and elementary propositional
logic (Chapter 3), I have presented the logic of terms and the logic
of propositions as complementary parts of one branch of study;

while in Chapter 4 I have tried to show how recognition of the inadequacy of the traditional analysis of propositions leads to a qualified acceptance of the modern calculus of predicates.

The chapters which follow these elementary expositions of logical systems are concerned with some of the philosophical problems that logic raises. After a general discussion of the nature of propositions and facts (Chapter 5), I have considered in some detail one widely-held view about the status of logical truths and their relation to rules of language (Chapter 6), and followed it up with an alternative view which seems to me preferable (Chapter 7). Chapter 8 is devoted to consideration of the notions of logical necessity and analyticity. The last chapter gives a brief and incomplete account of some kinds of thinking which only indirectly concern the formal logician. The main justification for its inclusion lies in the fact that, by crossing the boundaries of formal deductive logic, we can see more clearly where those boundaries lie.

Although I have expressed the arguments of this book as simply as I can, I have not attempted to be uncontroversial, even in the chapters which are mainly expository. The theories for and against which I have argued, though they are to be rejected if they are internally inconsistent, are not demonstrable. The questions discussed remain open questions and the answers which are suggested are of little value if they do not provoke the reader to a deeper investigation of the problems raised.

Of the many friends and colleagues who have helped me, directly or indirectly, in the writing of this book, I should like to thank, in particular, Professor H. J. Paton for his patient and unflagging interest and for many improvements in style and clarity, Mr E. J. Lemmon for many corrections, particularly in Chapters 2 and 3, Mr J. M. Hinton and Professor P. H. Nowell-Smith for their suggestions and encouragement, and Mr P. F. Strawson for the stimulus provided by his *Introduction to Logical Theory* which I have taken both as a model and as a challenge.

Oxford

June 1961   D. M.

1

LOGICAL FORM

Elementary logic is the study of the forms of valid argument and, more widely, of the different types of proposition which are logically true. Valid arguments usually consist of one set of propositions called 'premisses' and another set called 'conclusions'; and one of the logician's tasks is to make clear the conditions under which premisses 'entail' (or 'imply') conclusions, or, to put it in different words, conclusions 'follow logically' from premisses. He is concerned with logical truth, not with the 'material' truth or falsity of propositions. This distinction between logical and material truth is one that educated people make in ordinary language, whether or not they have studied logic. For we draw the distinction, consciously or unconsciously, when we use correctly such words as 'logic' and 'logical', which belong to common speech as well as to the vocabulary of a special study. It is a distinction which may easily be illustrated, however difficult it may be to explain fully.

It is true, as a matter of fact, that Eisenhower was in 1960 President of the United States of America, that King Charles I was beheaded, that common salt dissolves in water. It is true as a matter of logic, or 'logically true', that if no Protestant acknowledges the supremacy of the Pope, no one who acknowledges the supremacy of the Pope is a Protestant; that if Smith is a Marxist and if all Marxists are materialists, then Smith is a materialist; that if John always tells the truth, it is false that he ever tells lies. Some of the respects in which the first set of propositions differs from the second are apparent. If doubt were cast on any of the first set, we should know how to set about supporting them; we should appeal to observation and experiments, to the evidence of our senses. But we should not think of supporting any of the second set of propositions in the same way. Indeed we might well be puzzled if we were told that they were questioned at all, for, unlike the others, they seem to guarantee their own truth. We are tempted to say that the propositions of the first set *happen* to be true, while those in the second set *must* be true, or, in more technical language, that the first set consists of 'contingent', the second of 'necessary' propositions.

But here we must introduce a refinement. If we are to avoid the possibility of being misunderstood we should speak not of 'necessary' but of 'logically necessary' propositions. For all that logic can tell us, there may be other kinds of necessity than logical necessity, which is the notion which we are concerned to elucidate. That certain organisms die when deprived of oxygen might seem to be not something that just happens to be true but something that, in some sense, is necessarily true. But if this is so, the necessity is not logical but biological and, from the point of view of logic, the proposition is a contingent one. To contradict it might be to commit a mistake in biology; it would not be to make a logical error.

It is not difficult to list further respects in which the propositions of logic differ from 'factual' propositions. If we consider relatively uncomplicated logically true propositions, we notice that we do not need to be *informed* of their truth. Nor, if someone failed (or appeared to fail) to recognise their truth, should we feel any confidence that any instruction or information that we could give would dissolve his 'ignorance'. It seems inappropriate to say that we learn or remember or forget what propositions of logic are true, as we learn, remember and forget contingent propositions. Rather we *acknowledge* or *recognise* their truth, and failure to do so we attribute not to ignorance but to lack of comprehension. Logical truths are often both obvious and, so far as ordinary discourse is concerned, trivial. That the door of my college room is white is contingently true; that the door of my college room either is white or is not white is logically true but uninformative. It tells us no more than we knew already and what it does tell us seems for ordinary purposes to be not worth saying. At the same time, we are not inclined to dismiss all the propositions of logic as trivial tautologies, in the everyday sense of that word. Some we find worth saying even in ordinary life. "If John was the last person to visit my room and if the last visitor to my room

left the electric fire switched on, John must have left the fire on"
expresses a logically true proposition; but the conclusion expressed by
the consequent of this conditional sentence is one that a man might
fail to draw even though he had accepted the propositions expressed
by the antecedent as true. At least, the conclusion does not seem to be
a mere restatement of the premiss, as is the case in "If the door of
my room is white, the door of my room is white". Whether there is
any important distinction in kind between this pair of propositions
need not concern us here. It is enough that we should identify both
as examples of logically necessary, as opposed to contingent, propositions. But to say all this is not to provide an infallible criterion
for the identification of the propositions of logic; and perhaps the
most reliable rough indication that sentences are being used to
express logical statements is the occurrence in them of such words as
'so', 'therefore', 'consequently', 'it follows that', 'if ... then
...'—particularly when they are used in conjunction with words
that convey the notion of necessity, such as 'must', 'cannot',
'necessarily' and 'impossible'.

Logicians in the past have commonly defined logic as the study of
the forms of valid inference. It would be better to define it as the
study of the forms of true implication-propositions. To infer, in the
sense in which formal logicians are accustomed to use the word, is
to recognise what is implied.[1] We infer a valid conclusion from
premisses when we recognise that the premisses imply (or 'entail') the
conclusion. An inference, then, is an event in the life-history of a
rational being and as such may be of interest to a psychologist. But
logic is not psychology and is not a study of mental states, events or
activities: it is not concerned with my inference or yours from premisses to conclusions but, in so far as it considers particular arguments at all, with the validity of the steps and with the question of
whether or not the premisses entail the conclusions. To assert that
implication is the central topic of logic is to keep logic distinct from
psychology, which is the systematic study of the workings of the
mind.

A further advantage is gained too. When we say that premisses
imply a conclusion we do not commit ourselves to accepting either
premisses or conclusion as true; but when we claim to *infer* a certain

[1] On this point, see also p. 58.

conclusion from given premises, we commit ourselves to accepting both premises and conclusions as true. As we have seen already, the truth or falsity of particular non-logical propositions is no more the concern of pure logic than is the mental state of a participant in an argument. We *infer* a conclusion when we say, "All men are mortal and Socrates is a man; therefore Socrates is mortal". But the truth of the conclusion is not guaranteed by logic alone. For our inference to be a sound inference and for our argument to be a proof, the premises must be true; and that they are true cannot be established by logic. But it is a truth of logic that *if* all men are mortal and *if* Socrates is a man, *then* Socrates is mortal. If we restrict our attention to such statements as these, i.e. to true statements of implication, we exclude what is logically irrelevant, namely the truth or falsity of particular contingent statements.

Thus the central topic of logic is implication. But in saying this I do not intend to limit consideration only to those propositions in the expression of which the word 'imply' or its synonym 'entail' occurs. The relation of implication is expressed in many different ways and perhaps most commonly in sentences of the form 'if ... then (necessarily) ...'; and the reader is asked to understand the word 'implication' as intended to designate the relation in which one proposition or set of propositions stands to another proposition or set of propositions in those cases where the first cannot be true without the second also being true on logical grounds alone.

So far it has been said that logic is not concerned with the truth or falsity of the contingent propositions that constitute the premises and conclusions of particular arguments. There is a special reason for this. Logic is not concerned with the truth of individual arguments since it is not concerned, except for the purpose of illustrating general logical principles, with individual arguments at all. For logic, as was said at the beginning of this chapter, is the study of the *forms*, as opposed to the *subject-matter*, of logically true propositions. So let us examine this distinction between form and matter and see how it applies to logic.

Form and content

A school teacher fills in a child's report form with information about the child's progress. Until it is filled in, the form is blank and gives no factual information; it prescribes not what information shall be given but how it is to be presented. In the same way, we speak of forms of government (which determine not what laws are made but how they are made), the form of a sonnet (which is the framework within which a poet expresses himself). 'Shape', 'structure', 'frame', 'mould', 'pattern' suggest themselves as synonyms or near-synonyms of 'form'. The sentences, "Has he come?", "Is it raining?", "Where is the Post Office?" have different meanings but they are all alike in being questions. This likeness is a likeness of form and in distinguishing questions from commands, exhortations, assertions and expostulations we distinguish forms of utterance or forms of communication. If, however, we are to understand the forms with which the logician is concerned, we must draw a distinction that is not clearly marked in our ordinary language, namely that between a sentence and a proposition.

The question, "What did John say on that occasion?", is ambiguous. It can be an enquiry either about the exact words that John used on the occasion in question or about the substance or purport of what he said; in terms of our present distinction, it can ask either what the *sentence* was that John uttered or what the *proposition* was that he asserted. Sentences are grammatical or ungrammatical and consist of spoken or written words. Propositions are characterised as true or false and do not consist of words although they are expressed in words. The same proposition can be expressed in different sentences (e.g. "The King is dead", "Le roi est mort", "Der König ist tot"), while the same sentence can be used to express different propositions (as when you and I each say "I was born in London"). So a proposition is that which is (or could be) asserted to be the case, while sentences are the sets of words in which we express propositions. Not all sentences express propositions but only those of which it would be intelligible to say that their purport or sense was either true or false. Thus, for example, if one were to distinguish between the words that one uses when issuing a command and that which is commanded—and we do not need to decide if this is a useful or even a possible distinction—the distinction drawn would not be that between a sentence and a proposition. The word 'proposition' is restricted to that which can be asserted and can be true or false.

The distinction between sentences and propositions raises problems to which we shall return in a later chapter. But it is not an artificial distinction or one that, without absurdity, we could ignore or deny. If that which is asserted were not distinguishable from the words in which the assertion was expressed, it would be impossible for men who spoke in different languages to be aware of and consider the same truths. The Frenchman who says "Hitler est mort" would assert not the same but a different truth from that which the Englishman who says "Hitler is dead" asserts. But although the distinction belongs to common sense, common language is not equipped to express it unambiguously, and in order to mark it and prevent confusion I shall adopt an artificial device. When misunderstanding is likely to occur, I shall use sentences enclosed by *double* inverted commas to record the *sentences* themselves and sentences enclosed by *single* inverted commas to refer to the *propositions* which the quoted sentences would, according to standard usage, be used to express. Sometimes a more cumbersome but less artificial procedure will be followed; quoted words will be prefixed by the words 'the sentence' or 'the proposition'. But, where it is not stylistically awkward to do so, I shall avoid using quoted sentences to refer to propositions altogether and adopt such a locution as 'the proposition that Hitler is dead'. Thus ' "Hitler is dead" ', 'the proposition 'Hitler is dead' ' and 'the proposition that Hitler is dead' might be used as different ways of expressing the same thing.

It is with the forms of propositions and not the forms of sentences that logic is concerned. What in propositions is formal and what material may most readily be distinguished if we consider examples. Let us, then, first consider the pair of propositions

1. 'Tom is Australian'
2. 'Tom is not Australian'

2. is the contradictory of 1. If 1. is true, then, as a matter of logic, 2. must be false and *vice versa*. They cannot both be true together; they are *inconsistent* with each other. But what is there about them that makes them inconsistent? What explains the inconsistency is not the fact that it is Tom who is in question or that he is, or is not, Australian. Exactly the same sort of inconsistency would result if the

subject of the proposition were not Tom but Dick or Harry, and if it were his being Austrian or Armenian that was affirmed or denied. In other words the inconsistency is not to be explained by reference to the subject-matter of the propositions.

If we replace 'Tom' by S and 'Australian' by P and lay it down that S and P are to stand for any subject and any predicate whatsoever, we are left with two propositional frameworks or forms, 'S is P' and 'S is not P'. We can at once recognise that *any* pair of propositions of these forms will be inconsistent, provided that the letters S and P (which we may call 'term-variables') are taken to stand for the same subject and the same predicate when they occur in the same context. We can now say that any proposition of the form 'S is P' is inconsistent with the corresponding proposition of the form 'S is not P' or, in words that involve no special symbolism, any proposition in which a predicate is asserted of a subject is necessarily inconsistent with the corresponding proposition in which the same predicate is denied of the subject. Whether we express our conclusions in the first way or in the second, we assert the same truth, that the inconsistency of the two propositions is to be explained by reference not to their content but to their forms. What the two forms of propositions are, we can express either in a terminology which involves no special signs or, less cumbersomely, in a special notation.

But though the proposition 'Tom is Australian' is correctly analysed as of the form, 'S is P', by which, as I have said, we are to understand that it is a proposition in which a predicate is asserted of a subject, it is also of a simpler form. Compare 1. and 2. with the pair of propositions

3. 'There is a God'
4. 'There is no God'

These, like 1. and 2., are contradictories and inconsistent with each other. Yet they do not exemplify the forms, 'S is P' and 'S is not P'. It is not the case here that a predicate is asserted or denied of a subject. What they have in common with 1. and 2. is the fact that they are a pair of propositions one member of which is the contradictory or negation of the other. This consideration has led logicians to adopt a briefer and simpler formal notation, whereby the letters 'p', 'q', 'r' etc. are used to stand for any proposition whatsoever, while 'not-p', 'not-q', 'not-r' etc. stand for their corresponding negations. Thus both 'Tom is Australian' and 'There is a God' exemplify the form 'p', with their contradictories exemplifying the form 'not-p'. This simpler notation enables us to express a logical truth of greater generality than we could express in either the language or the special notation which we originally used to represent the forms, and to display the logical relationship of, 'Tom is Australian' and 'Tom is not Australian'. Thus, 'Tom is Australian' exemplifies the form 'p' and at the same time the sub-form 'S is P', since it is a proposition in which something is asserted of (or predicated of) a subject. But if all that concerns us is to explain the logical relationship in which it stands to 'Tom is not Australian', we need only recognise that it is of the form 'p'.

Form and validity

We have now reached a point where we can consider the relation between the forms of logically true (or false) propositions and their logical truth (or falsity). To see that only the form and not the subject-matter of particular contradictory propositions is relevant to their mutual inconsistency is to recognise the point of saying that they are inconsistent because of their form. When we say, without thought of the technicalities of logical analysis, that what somebody said is inconsistent since he contradicted himself, we in fact refer to formal characteristics of his statements in order to explain their inconsistency.[1] Indeed, so close is the relation between the forms of propositions and their logical truth or validity that there is a temptation to *define* the form of a logically necessary proposition, or a sound argument, as that in virtue of which the proposition is logically necessary or valid. But it is not difficult to see why this temptation must be resisted. For if we were to say that arguments are valid in virtue of their form and to add that we *mean* by 'form' that in virtue of which arguments are valid, we should have succeeded in

[1] To say that logic is the study of implication suggests that the only logical relationship between propositions is the relation of implication. We should notice, then, that to say that a proposition of the form 'p' is inconsistent with the corresponding proposition of the form 'not-p' is to say something that can be equally well expressed as a statement of implication, namely, 'that a proposition of the form p is true implies that the corresponding proposition of the form not-p is false'.

saying no more than that arguments are valid in virtue of that in virtue of which they are valid. What we have seen is not an empty truism but the fact that at least one very general type of inconsistency that holds between propositions is partly to be explained by reference to the structure, and not the subject-matter, of those propositions. But, it must be admitted, this conclusion can only be illuminating if the distinction between form and matter can be established without covert recourse to the circular account of form which we have rejected. It is to be hoped that we have gone some way towards clarifying this distinction to which later we shall have occasion to return.

Although it is easy to see that there is a close connection between the validity of arguments and their logical form, it is not easy to state with precision what that relation is. How far (if at all) are we entitled to say that a given argument is valid because of or in virtue of its form? We might be tempted to say that the argument, 'If Tom is Australian then it is false that he is not Australian', is valid 1. because it is of the form, 'if *p*, then not *not-p*', and 2. because it is a law that arguments of that form are valid. And we might be inclined to express our reasoning thus:

> Argument A is of the form F
> Arguments of the form F are valid
> ∴ Argument A is valid

But this will not do. It suggests that in order to know that the given concrete argument is valid we need *first* to know that arguments of the given form are valid. And this is false. For I do not need to recognise the logical law that, whatever proposition '*p*' may be, if *p*, then not *not-p*, as a precondition for seeing that if Tom is Australian it must be false that he is not Australian. A man might well recognise that this must be so without recognising anything further about the structure of the argument. Again, he might have a deeper insight and not only recognise the argument as valid but also see that its validity was formal (i.e. that only the formal features of the argument, as distinct from its content, were relevant to its validity). Thirdly, he might go still further and recognise that the argument, being formally valid, was generalisable (i.e. that it exemplified a general logical law). In such a case we proceed *to* the general law: we do not start *from* the general law and deduce its consequences in a given case. We do not need to know the laws of logic, or even that there are such laws, in order to distinguish sound from unsound argument. The unqualified assertion that particular arguments are valid in virtue of their forms appears to commit us to the denial of this unquestionable truth and must therefore be rejected. All that we are entitled to say is that a given argument is valid *as being of* a given form and that to explain the validity of an argument by reference to its form is to display it as an exemplification of a formal logical law.

It is to be noticed, further, that in recognising a given argument as an exemplification of a given form of argument, we throw no light on the fact that arguments of that form are valid. To draw attention to the fact that 'If Tom is Australian, it is false that he is not Australian' exemplifies the formal law, 'For any *p*, if *p*, then not *not-p*', in no way explains why 'For any *p*, if *p*, then not *not-p*' is a law of logic. The law can be understood as stating that propositions of a given form are necessarily true. I do not explain why propositions of that form are necessarily true by saying 'because they are of that form'. It would be no more helpful to say *that*, than to say that true statements are true because they are true. If I am asked to prove that what I claim to be a law is indeed a law, two courses only are open to me: I may claim either that the law is indemonstrable and self-evident or that it follows from other laws of logic that are accepted as indemonstrable or self-evident. It is only to explain the necessity of particular, concrete arguments that I can appeal to the notion of form.

Of course nothing has been said so far that entitles us to conclude that all logic is formal. We are clearly not justified in arguing that because pairs of propositions are inconsistent if they are contradictory in form, all examples of inconsistency and logical necessity are to be explained by reference to the formal characteristics of propositions, and in a later chapter we shall have occasion to consider the possibility of non-formal logic. What makes it possible for us to generalise about the relation of form to logical necessity is the fact that, in more than two thousand years, logicians have succeeded in showing that the relationship holds over a very wide range of arguments.

The logic of propositions and the logic of terms

So far we have seen that, in order to display the logical relationship in which contradictory propositions stand to one another, it is unnecessary to represent in our formulae their *internal* structure. When propositions are simple contradictories, it is logically irrelevant whether they are predicative (like 'Tom is Australian') or existential (like 'There is a God'). They are adequately represented as '*p*', '*q*', '*r*', '*not-p*', '*not-q*', '*not-r*' etc. By means of these propositional variables we can state the general logical law, 'Not both *p* and *not-p*'. This is called the Law of Non-Contradiction and is one of three so-called Laws of Thought which traditionally were regarded as, in some special but ill-defined ways, basic. The other members of the trio, the Law of Identity, that if a proposition is true it is true, and the Law of Excluded Middle, that every proposition is either true or false, can also be expressed in the same notation, as 'If *p*, then *p*' ('*p* implies *p*') and 'Either *p* or *not-p*'. The systematic study of all such laws, that is to say of all the laws of logic for the formulation of which the internal structure of propositions can be neglected, constitutes what is called 'the logic of propositions', or, more illuminatingly, the logic of elementary propositions. This branch of logic has been fully explored only in the last sixty or seventy years.

But there are other logical laws which can be expressed only in a formal notation which is equipped to represent the internal structure of propositions. For example, the apparatus of elementary propositional variables is not adequate to display the logic of 'If none of the delegates was a communist, then no communist was a delegate'. If we substitute '*p*' for 'none of the delegates were communists' and '*q*' for 'no communists were delegates' we arrive at the formula, 'if *p*, then *q*', which is manifestly not a law of logic. It is self-evidently false that *any* one proposition ('*p*') implies *any* other proposition ('*q*'). In order to display the logical structure of this argument we need 'term-variables', e.g. *X* and *Y* or *S* and *P*, from which we can construct the formula, 'If no *X* is *Y*, then no *Y* is *X*', in which *X* and *Y* stand for any subject-term and any predicate-term.[1] This is readily seen to be a general logical law which could be expressed at

[1] For an explanation of 'term', see p. 25.

greater length as 'For all X and for all Y, where X and Y are terms related as subject and predicate, if no X is Y, then necessarily no Y is X'. The systematic study of the forms of argument for the exposition of which it is necessary that propositions should be analysed into subjects and predicates, is called the 'logic of terms'. It was the first branch of logic to be fully developed and constitutes the body of what is called traditional logic.

The forms of sentences and the forms of propositions

When the forms of the propositions, 'All men are mortal' and 'No man (men) is (are) mortal', are represented as 'All X is Y' and 'No X is Y', it might be thought that the words 'all', 'is', 'no' are the residue of the sentences which is left when we substitute X and Y for the subject-matter words, 'man' and 'mortal'. But this would be a mistake. Propositions are not sentences, and the elements of propositions and of the *forms* of propositions are not words. The function of the word 'all' in the formula is simply to mark the fact that Y is predicable of (is capable of being asserted of) whatever is X, no matter what linguistic device is used to express that function. The same proposition can be expressed in English or in any other language in an indefinitely large number of ways, only a few of which involve the use of the English word 'all'. Similarly, the function of 'is' is to mark the fact that Y is predicable of X (or X of Y); and, in this mixed notation, which comprises English words as well as letters of the alphabet, 'All X is Y' and 'No X is Y' are to be understood as giving the forms of any propositions in which anything is asserted or denied of the whole of a subject. Thus 'Tigers eat meat' and 'Children should be seen and not heard' (in which it is asserted of all tigers that they eat meat and of all children that they 'should-be-seen-and-not-heard') are of the form, 'All X is Y', as much as 'All salt is soluble in water' or 'All men are mortal'. Misunderstanding is unlikely to arise so long as we bear in mind the fact that logic investigates not the forms of sentences but the forms of propositions. "Tigers eat meat" and "All tigers are carnivorous" are sentences that can be interpreted as expressing the same thought, the form of which, as we have seen, is traditionally represented as 'All X is Y' (or 'All S is P').

It is interesting to observe that Aristotle's selection of a formal

vocabulary suggests that he also was concerned to prevent confusion between grammatical and logical form. To mark the relation
between subject and predicate, in his formula for a proposition, he
used two Greek words that were not commonly so used in ordinary
speech and were clearly intended as technical. Thus his version of
"All *A* is *B*", literally translated, is "*B* belongs to all *A*" or "*B* is
predicated of all *A*". He was apparently concerned to emphasise the
fact (which might have been missed had he adopted the expression
"*A is B*") that, for a proposition to be of this form, it need not be
expressed in any particular verbal form. Similarly he said "we
ought" (i.e. in our formularisations of arguments) "to exchange
equivalent terms, words for words and phrases for phrases". The
point of this remark is brought out by an early commentator on
Aristotle who said that what makes a syllogism a syllogism is not
the words used but their meanings.[1]

Since a formula such as 'All *X* is *Y*' expresses the form of
propositions and not of the enormous range of possible sentences in
all languages which can be used to express them, we cannot mean,
when we say that two propositions are of the same form, that they
are expressed in sentences that look or sound similar. It is not
surprising, however, that in general the grammatical forms of
expression reveal the structure of the thoughts or propositions
which they are used to express, and no doubt general syntactical
similarities led the pioneers of logic to the recognition of formal
identities in the structure of propositions, which makes the systematic
study of logic possible.

A corollary of the view that the formulae of logic do not represent the structure of sentences is that they cannot be used as criteria
for deciding if given sentences in ordinary language are or are not
being used to express propositions of the forms in question. Living
languages do not conform to rigid and unalterable rules and there is
no one constant form of words in which a given proposition must
be expressed. This is not to deny that there is always a standard
vocabulary and standard usage—indeed if there were not, complete
communication would be impossible; but the rules of standard
speech are not free from exceptions, and considerable irregularity

[1] On the points raised in this paragraph, see J. Łukasiewicz, *Aristotle's
Syllogistic*, 1951, ch. 1.

in grammar and vocabulary is compatible with intelligibility. Thus, though we often speak without qualification of *the* meaning of a sentence, there is no immutable correlation between words and meanings, or between particular sentences and particular propositions. Very roughly, 'the meaning of a sentence' is what most people (or people who speak 'correctly') would use the sentence to convey. In order to decide if an argument expressed in English sentences is valid or of what form it is, we must first understand the sentences, that is to say, grasp what propositions they were intended to express. In that task the formulae of logic give us no assistance. Although one of the achievements of modern logic is to have devised simple mechanical methods for determining if certain propositions are contingent, logically necessary or logically impossible, these tests can be applied only after sentences are understood and the corresponding propositions expressed in the appropriate logical notation.

Although a particular argument may be valid in that it possesses certain formal features, it is clearly not necessary, as we have seen, that we should *know* that it possesses those features before recognising it as valid. Formal logic isolates the structure of propositions of logical necessity: it does not *prescribe* what forms are to be considered acceptable. The starting point for logic is our ability to distinguish sound from unsound reasoning, consistent from inconsistent propositions, and to this the formal logician appeals. He does not invent principles of argument but discovers them and draws them to our attention. He also has the task of devising notations in which the forms of arguments are perspicuously displayed. This demands insight and inventiveness and on its successful accomplishment most advances in logical analysis depend. It was the recognition more than two thousand years ago that a very wide range of propositions are of a form that can be represented symbolically as '*B* belongs to *A*' (or '*X* is *Y*' or '*S* is *P*') that made systematic logical analysis possible. The formal analysis of such propositions is now so familiar to us that it requires imagination to realise that it was a discovery at all. But it is to be compared in importance with the invention of the sign '0', to signify zero, which transformed arithmetic and created entirely fresh possibilities for its development. Whereas a system of shorthand enables us to record speech in an abbreviated form, a good logical notation equips us to analyse the forms of propositions and arguments. To have constructed a completely adequate one is to have mastered the structure of logical relationships.

As we have seen, the fact that a proposition is of a certain form does not preclude it from being at the same time of another more general or more specific form. 'Tom is Australian' exemplifies the form 'p' and also 'X is Y'. 'Elliot ran faster than Hewson' is of three forms. First, it exemplifies 'p' in that it is a proposition that is true or false; secondly, it exemplifies 'X is Y', for of Elliot it is predicated that he ran-faster-than-Hewson; thirdly, it is a proposition in which 'Elliot' and 'Hewson' are related terms—but not related as subject and predicate.[1] When we speak of *the* logical form of a proposition we usually refer to the form which it possesses that is relevant to the logical relationship in which it stands to other propositions in a given context. Thus we should say that 'Elliot ran faster than Hewson' is of the form 'p' when considered in relation to its contradictory, 'Elliot did not run faster than Hewson'; that it is of the form 'X is Y' when it is considered as a premiss in the syllogistic argument, 'Anybody who ran faster than Hewson broke the world record for the mile and Elliot ran faster than Hewson, so Elliot broke the world record'; that it is of another, as yet unidentified, relational form when considered as a premiss of the argument, 'Elliot ran faster than Hewson and Hewson ran faster than Thomas, so Elliot ran faster than Thomas'.

[1] For further discussion of the logic of non-predicative relations, see ch. 7.

THE TRADITIONAL LOGIC OF TERMS

The earliest system of logic which has survived was formulated by Aristotle in the fourth century B.C., and for most of the last two thousand years it has been considered authoritative and in need of no more than minor modifications. Although, at the present time, few philosophers would claim that it—with the accretions which it has acquired since Aristotle's time—is complete, and although many of its doctrines and assumptions are now generally considered mistaken or misleading, the 'traditional system' is the natural starting-point for logical enquiry. From this Aristotelian tradition we inherit, not only the vocabulary of logic (e.g. the distinction between 'form' and 'matter' and such words as 'inference', 'implication', 'proposition', 'premiss', 'conclusion' and 'logic' itself), but also the conceptual framework of a great part of later European philosophical and scientific thought.

The central concern of traditional logic is the investigation of the logical relations of four propositional forms—Universal Affirmative (A), Universal Negative (E), Particular Affirmative (I), Particular Negative (O), which may be represented and exemplified as follows:

A	All S is P	All men are mortal
E	No S is P	No men are mortal
I	Some S is P	Some men are mortal
O	Some S is not P	Some men are not mortal

It was traditionally assumed that all propositions are of subject-predicate form, that is to say that every proposition has a subject of which something is predicated (or said about it). S stands for the subject-term, P for the predicate-term, and 'is' (the 'copula') marks the fact that P is to be taken as predicated of S. The distinction between affirmative and negative is called a distinction of Quality; the distinction between universal and particular a distinction of Quantity. Although Aristotle discusses singular propositions, i.e. propositions about individuals, he did not consider patterns of inference in which they play a part in his major logical writings. Singular propositions such as 'Socrates is mortal' were, for a reason which we shall see later, traditionally considered to exemplify the A form.

The syllogism

Inference, for traditional logic, is either 'immediate' or 'mediate'. We make an immediate inference when we infer a valid conclusion from a single premiss of S-P (subject-predicate) form, a mediate inference when we infer from two premisses in which there is one 'middle term' to a conclusion. The principal type of inference with which traditional logic is concerned is the syllogism, and this we shall consider first.

A syllogism is an argument with two premisses and a conclusion; each of the three propositions which constitute the premisses and conclusion are of one of the four forms, A, E, I or O; the argument contains three 'terms'. By 'terms' are meant those constituents or elements of propositions that are not themselves propositions and are not expressed by the copula or the signs of quality or quantity ('all', 'some', 'no', 'not').

In the proposition, 'All men are mortal', 'men' and 'mortal' are subject- and predicate-terms respectively. Since a proposition is not the sentence which is used to express it, the terms of a proposition are not to be identified with the words or some of the words which make up the sentence. A term is rather the sense of the word or phrase in a sentence that is used to express that which the proposition is about (the subject) and that which is predicated of it.

Aristotle himself defines a syllogism as "a discourse in which, certain things being stated, something other than what is stated follows of necessity from their being so", but the word is applied more narrowly by all logicians (including Aristotle) than this definition would lead us to expect. It is restricted to arguments satisfying the conditions which I have given in which, by virtue of the fact that one of the three terms, the *middle* term, is identical in both premisses, a connection is inferred, validly or invalidly, between the other two terms. Let us consider an example:

>All professors are learned
>Some Scotsmen are professors
>∴ Some Scotsmen are learned

In this syllogism, 'professors' is the middle term and its connection with 'learned' in one premiss and with 'Scotsmen' in the other necessitates a connection, propounded in the conclusion, between those other two terms. The predicate-term in the conclusion is called the 'major term' and the premiss in which it occurs is the 'major premiss'. The premiss in which the subject-term of the conclusion (the 'minor term') occurs is called the 'minor premiss'. Since the relation between premisses and conclusion is timeless (for example, the major premiss does not 'occur' in time *before* the minor premiss), it is logically irrelevant in what order we choose to expound the premisses of a syllogism. The form of the above syllogism may conveniently be symbolised as follows:

>All M is P
>Some S is M
>∴ Some S is P

If we consider this schema and ignore the signs of Quantity and Quality we can see that there are only four possible arrangements of the terms, granted that the conclusion must be S-P and that the order of the premisses is irrelevant.

I	II	III	IV
MP	PM	MP	PM
SM	SM	MS	MS
SP	SP	SP	SP

These four schemata are called the four 'Figures' of syllogism and they are numbered in the order given.

It can be seen that, on the assumption that each of the premisses can be of any one of the four forms, A, E, I and O, $4 \times 4 \times 4$ (i.e. 64) possible schemata, which are called 'moods', can be constructed for each figure. Thus the total number of possible schemata for all four figures is 256. But there are not 256 forms of valid syllogism. It is intuitively obvious, for example, that there could be no valid inference of the form,

$$\text{All } M \text{ is } P$$
$$\text{All } S \text{ is } M$$
$$\therefore \text{ No } S \text{ is } P$$

Indeed of the 256 possible combinations of trios of subject-predicate propositions involving three terms, twenty-four only are valid moods. And we do not need the help of logical text-books to discover which these are. It is possible for us to distinguish them from the invalid moods, by considering each combination in turn, and 'seeing' whether an argument of that form would or would not be valid. In fact if, after the most careful consideration, we 'saw' to be valid a mood which a text-book ruled to be invalid, we should have to abandon the text-book or the study of logic. For, as has already been said, the starting point of logic is our ability to distinguish sound from unsound reasoning. At the same time, however, we can achieve the same result more easily and systematically by referring to the so-called rules of the syllogism which state succinctly the general conditions to which we can see that syllogisms must conform if they are to be valid.

The general rules for the syllogism lay down the necessary, indeed sufficient, conditions that any syllogism, whatever may be the position of the middle term, must satisfy if it is to be valid. They comprise rules of distribution and rules of quality and quantity. But before they are listed it will be convenient to explain briefly what is meant by the phrase, 'the distribution of terms'.

The distribution of terms

A term is said to be distributed if it is used in its widest generality, undistributed if its use is either explicitly restricted to less than it can be applied to or is indeterminate. Thus, in the proposition, 'All men are mortal', the term 'men' is distributed; in fact we may say that the function of 'all' is to distribute it. It conveys that what is predicated is predicated of the whole *extension* of 'men' (where the *extension* of a term consists of the range of things to which the term is applicable). Similarly the subject-term of an E proposition is distributed, for the predicate is denied of its whole extension. It is clear that in 'Some men are mortal' and 'Some men are not mortal' the term 'men' is undistributed. It is not so easy to grasp the notion of the distribution of predicate-terms. The term 'immortal' in 'No men are immortal' is distributed, since in the proposition the complete extension of 'immortal' (i.e. the total range of things that are immortal) is excluded from the range of things that are men. Similarly, in 'Some men are not immortal', we exclude the total extension of 'immortal' from 'some men'. The predicate-terms of both A and I propositions are undistributed; if we say either that all men are mortal or that some men are mortal, we neither assert nor deny that other things than men are also mortal.

Although the doctrine of distribution is neither clear nor philosophically unobjectionable, it is convenient to retain it in an elementary exposition of formal logic. To reject it would necessitate the reformulation of much of traditional doctrine. Hence we shall keep it as a device for expounding the logical relations of propositions of the four traditional forms. We can display the distribution of terms in a table:

All *S* is *P*	*S* distributed	*P* undistributed
No *S* is *P*	*S* distributed	*P* distributed
Some *S* is *P*	*S* undistributed	*P* undistributed
Some *S* is not *P*	*S* undistributed	*P* distributed

We are now equipped to consider the rules for the syllogism.

Rules of distribution

1. The middle term must be distributed in at least one premiss.
2. A term that is distributed in the conclusion must be distributed in the corresponding premisses.

Rules of quality and quantity

3. At least one premiss must be affirmative.
4. If one premiss is negative, the conclusion must be negative.
5. If both premisses are affirmative, the conclusion must be affirmative.
6. One premiss at least must be universal.
7. If one premiss is particular, the conclusion must be particular.

8. If the major premiss is particular, the minor premiss cannot be negative.

The necessity for each of these rules can readily be recognised.

Rule 1: If the middle term is undistributed, then, in each of the premisses, it may apply to different parts or members of the same whole. If some men are jealous and some men are bad-tempered, it does not follow that some jealous people are bad-tempered. That the men who are jealous are different men from those who are bad-tempered is compatible with the two given propositions.

Rule 2: In other words, a term cannot be used in wider generality in the conclusion than in its corresponding premiss. If all blue-eyed men are blond and some Danes are blue-eyed, it does not follow that all Danes are blond, only that some are.

Rule 3: A negative proposition separates its terms. If both premisses were negative, both S and P would be separated from M and no conclusion about the relation of S to P could be drawn. If no students in the First Class were biochemists and no members of Judas College were in the First Class, we can draw no conclusion about the presence or absence of biochemists at Judas College.

Rule 4: If a relation is affirmed between X and Y but denied between Y and Z, then, if any conclusion can be drawn, it must be one denying the relation between X and Z.

Rule 5: The fact that X and Z are each related affirmatively with Y cannot entitle us to conclude that they are negatively related to each other.

Rules 6, 7 and 8 are corollaries of Rules 1–5 and can therefore be proved from them.[1]

By applying these rules to the sixty-four possible combinations of propositions in each figure, we find that there are eleven capable of yielding valid syllogisms, namely AAA, AII, AAI, IAI, EAE, AEE, EAO, AEO, AOO, OAO, EIO. But since there are, as we have seen (p. 26), four possible arrangements of subject-, predicate- and middle-terms (i.e. four figures), the possibility is left open that each of these eleven forms will be valid in each figure. This, however, is not the case. In Figure II, for example, where the middle term is predicate in both premisses, no forms will be valid in which both premisses are

[1] For proofs of those rules, see e.g. L. S. Stebbing, *A Modern Elementary Logic*, revised ed., 1952, pp. 56 and 57.

affirmative, since the predicate terms of affirmative propositions are undistributed, and, by Rule 1, the middle term must be distributed at least once. By referring to the general rules and to the table of distribution, we can, in fact, deduce whether any of the eleven combinations yields a valid mood in any given figure. But the process of elimination has been simplified by the formulation of special rules which are specifications of the general rules as they are applicable to each figure.

Special rules for Figure I

I.1. The minor premiss must be affirmative.

I.2. The major premiss must be universal.

I shall not give proofs for all the special rules. Proofs for I.1. and I.2. will serve as examples.

Proof for I.1. If the minor premiss were negative, the major premiss would be affirmative (Rule 3) and the conclusion negative (Rule 4). But then the major term would be distributed in the conclusion but not in the major premiss (Table of Distribution). This is impossible (Rule 2). The minor premiss must therefore be affirmative.

Proof of I.2. Since the minor premiss is affirmative (I.1.), the middle term, which is its predicate, is undistributed in it (Table of Distribution). Therefore the middle term must be distributed as subject of the major premiss (Rule 1), which must therefore be universal (Table of Distribution).

By reference to these two special rules, we can now determine which of the eleven combinations yield valid moods in Figure 1:

> AEE, AEO and AOO are excluded by I.1.
> IAI and OAO are excluded by I.2.
> AAA, EAE, AII, EIO, AAI, EAO are valid moods.

Special rules for Figure II

II.1. One premiss must be negative.

II.2. The major premiss must be universal.

> AAA, AAI, AII, IAI are excluded by II.1.
> OAO is excluded by II.2.
> EAE, AEE, EIO, AOO, EAO, AEO are valid moods.

Special rules for Figure III

III.1. The minor premiss must be affirmative.

III.2. The conclusion must be particular.

> AEE, AEO and AOO are excluded by III.1.
> AAA and EAE are excluded by III.2.
> AAI, IAI, AII, EAO, OAO, EIO are valid moods.

Special rules for Figure IV

IV.1. The major premiss cannot be particular if either premiss is negative.

IV.2. The minor premiss cannot be particular if the major premiss is affirmative.

IV.3. The conclusion cannot be universal if the minor premiss is affirmative.

> OAO is excluded by IV.1.
> AII and AOO are excluded by IV.2.
> AAA and EAE are excluded by IV.3.
> AAI, AEE, IAI, EAO, EIO, AEO are valid moods.

Thus the valid moods in all figures are:

  I. AAA, EAE, AII, EIO, [AAI], [EAO].
 II. EAE, AEE, EIO, AOO, [EAO], [AEO].
III. AAI, IAI, AII, EAO, OAO, EIO.
 IV. AAI, AEE, IAI, EAO, EIO, [AEO].

The moods printed in square brackets are *weakened* or *subaltern* moods. Their conclusions are less general than the conclusions that can be drawn from the same premisses. If A implies I (a doctrine of traditional logic which will be discussed later), then 'All men are mortal' (A) and 'All Greeks are men' (A) imply 'All Greeks are mortal' (A), and also the *weaker* conclusion 'Some Greeks are mortal' (I).

The mood names that medieval logicians gave to the nineteen unweakened valid moods are still commonly used in textbooks:

Figure I   Barbara, Celarent, Darii, Ferio
Figure II   Cesare, Camestres, Festino, Baroko

Figure III Darapti, Disamis, Datisi, Felapton, Bokardo, Ferison
Figure IV Bramantip, Camenes, Dimaris, Fesapo, Fresison

It will be clear that the rules of the syllogism are negative. They enable us to eliminate invalid moods. But to do so is not in itself to prove that the moods that satisfy the rules are in fact valid. Before we consider the methods of proof that Aristotle adopted to achieve this object, it is necessary to review the laws of immediate inference which are assumed in the proofs. These are the laws of conversion and the laws of the square of opposition.

The square of opposition

The formal relations of propositions with identical terms of the four forms, A, E, I and O, were represented by traditional logicians by a diagram called the square of opposition.

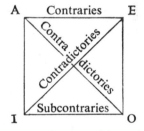

The diagram represents the opposition of propositions of the four forms to one another. Two propositions having the same terms are said to be *opposed* to each other if they differ in quantity or quality or both quantity and quality. A and E are *contraries* and contrary propositions are defined as those pairs of universal propositions which differ in quality but not in quantity. I and O are *subcontraries*. They are particular propositions which differ in quality. A and E are the *contradictories* respectively of O and I. I and O differ from A and E respectively in quantity and are called the *subalterns* of A and E. As for the relations of logical necessity in which propositions of the four forms stand to one another, contraries cannot both be true together, though they can both be false; thus 'if A, then necessarily not-E', but not 'if not-A, then necessarily E'. By contrast, subcontraries can both be true together but cannot both be false. Contradictories cannot be true or false together: if A is true, O must be false; if A is false, O must be true; if E is true, I must be false; if E is false, I must be true. A implies I and E implies O; thus if all men are mortal, then necessarily some men are mortal; and if no men are mortal, some men are not mortal.

We may express the traditional doctrine of the relations of the A, E, I and O forms in tabular form:

	A	E	I	O
A true	T	F	T	F
A false	F	U	U	T
E true	F	T	F	T
E false	U	F	T	U
I true	U	F	T	U
I false	F	T	F	T
O true	F	U	U	T
O false	T	F	T	F

T = True   F = False   U = Undetermined

If we start at the top of the left-hand column and read along the line, we get, 'If A is true, then A is true, E is false, I is true and O is false'.

If we accept this account of the logical relations of A, E, I and O propositions, possessing the same terms, we shall also accept A as equivalent to Not-O and E as equivalent to Not-I, in that Not-O is the contradictory of the contradictory of A, while Not-I is the contradictory of the contradictory of E.

Immediate inferences

Traditional logicians recognised two operations on propositions which yield further propositions which can validly and *immediately* (i.e. without the mediation of a middle term) be inferred from the original propositions. These operations are *conversion* and *obversion*. There are in addition complex operations which consist in both

2+

converting and obverting the same proposition. Although only conversion is involved in syllogistic proofs, it will be convenient to list the other forms of immediate inference accepted by post-Aristotelian traditional logicians.[1]

Conversion: We convert a proposition when we transpose the terms of the original proposition. There are two kinds of conversion, *simple* conversion and conversion *per accidens*. When we transpose the terms of the original proposition, leaving its quantity unchanged, we perform a simple conversion. The simple conversion of E and I propositions is valid and the resulting propositions (the converses) are logically equivalent to the original propositions (the convertends); that is to say, the convertend is true if and only if the converse is true or, in other words, each implies the other. Thus, 'No Chinese have curly hair' is the simple converse of 'No curly-haired people are Chinese', and 'Some politicians are corrupt' of 'Some corrupt people are politicians'. The simple conversion of an A proposition is invalid: from 'All men are mortal' one cannot validly infer 'All mortals are men'. But an A proposition can be converted *per accidens*: its converse is an I proposition. Thus from 'All men are mortal' we may infer, by conversion *per accidens*, 'Some mortals are men'. We cannot infer from I to A, nor can O propositions be converted at all.

Obversion: We obvert a proposition when we change its quality and negate the predicate-term. Propositions of all four forms can be validly obverted and the obverted propositions (the obverses) are logically equivalent to the obvertends.

> All *S* is *P* obverts to No *S* is *not-P*
> Some *S* is *P*   ,,   ,, Some *S* is not *not-P*
> No *S* is *P*   ,,   ,, All *S* is *not-P*
> Some *S* is not *P* ,,   ,, Some *S* is *not-P*

Contraposition is the operation of converting the obverse of a proposition or of obverting its converse. The predicate of the original proposition becomes the subject of the resulting proposition. Thus from 'No athletic people are intellectual' we obtain 'All athletic people are non-intellectual' (obversion) and thence 'Some non-intellectuals are athletic' (conversion).

[1] Negative terms, e.g. '*not-P*', were not admitted by Aristotle.

Inversion: The inverse of a proposition is a proposition which can be inferred from it and which has as its subject the contradictory of the original subject. Thus the inverse of 'All scholars are diligent' (A) is 'Some non-scholars are non-diligent', while the inverse of 'No scholars are lazy' (E) is 'Some non-scholars are lazy'. The steps by which the inverse is reached can be shown in a table:

1. All S is P
2. No S is *not-P* (obverse of 1)
3. No *not-P* is S (converse of 2)
4. All *not-P* is *not-S* (obverse of 3)
5. Some *not-S* is *not-P* (converse *per accidens* of 3)

Few will be prepared to accept as a proof of immortality the fact that, according to traditional doctrine, the valid inverse of 'All men are mortal' is 'Some not-men are immortal'. How is it that what appear, at first sight, to be valid steps lead to consequences as unacceptable as this? The weak link in the chain is the operation of conversion *per accidens*, whereby we pass from 'All S is P' to 'Some P is S'. Now it is a *precondition* of some X's being Y that there are X's. This being so, 'All S is P' can imply 'Some P is S' (conversion *per accidens*) as well as 'Some S is P' (Square of Opposition), only if it is a precondition for all S being P that there are both instances of S and instances of P. But it is *not* a precondition of universal propositions that their predicate terms and their negations are in fact instantiated, whatever may be true of subject-terms; if no men are immortal, it does not follow that some other things *are* immortal. For this reason, the inference from 'All scholars are diligent' to the inverse 'Some who are not scholars are not diligent', though sanctioned by traditional logic, is invalid. This defect in the traditional system will be considered later.

Of the forms of immediate inference, only conversion is of permanent logical interest. It is doubtful if, when we obvert, we do more than substitute one sentence for another, both of which express the same proposition. The solution to this problem turns on the answer that is given to the question whether "S is *not-P*" and "S is not P" express the same proposition. If the function of "S is *not-P*" is simply to negate 'S is P', then it is logically indistinguishable from

"*S* is not *P*". We do not eliminate negative propositions by the verbal device of linking a predicate word and 'not' by a hyphen.

We are now in a position to review the procedure adopted by Aristotle to prove the validity of the syllogistic moods.

The reduction of syllogisms

Aristotle distinguished two kinds of syllogism, *perfect* and *imperfect*. "I call that a perfect syllogism," he says, "which needs nothing other than what has been stated to make plain what necessarily follows; a syllogism is imperfect, if it needs either one or more propositions which are indeed the necessary consequences of the terms set down, but have not been expressly stated by the premisses."[1] He considered unweakened syllogisms of the first figure (Barbara, Celarent, Darii, Ferio) to be perfect, all the rest imperfect. The procedure called *reduction* is that of deducing the valid imperfect moods from the perfect moods.[2]

Reduction is of two kinds, *direct* and *indirect*. All of the valid imperfect moods except two are directly reduced; Baroko (Figure II) and Bokardo (Figure III) are indirectly reduced.

Direct reduction: Many of the moods are logically equivalent to one another, and often a syllogism can be transformed by simple conversion of one or more of its component propositions and by altering the order of the premisses. Thus since E and I propositions are convertible, EIO which is valid in the first figure is valid also in each of the other three.

I Ferio	II Festino	III Ferison	IV Fresison
No *M* is *P*	No *P* is *M*	No *M* is *P*	No *P* is *M*
Some *S* is *M*	Some *S* is *M*	Some *M* is *S*	Some *M* is *S*
∴ Some *S* is not *P*	Some *S* is not *P*	Some *S* is not *P*	Some *S* is not *P*

In all of these moods both the major premisses and the minor premisses are logically equivalent. Reduction of the second, third and

[1] *Prior Analytics*, 24b.

[2] Although Aristotle considered all four unweakened moods of the first figure as perfect and, hence, requiring no proof, he recognised that the two moods with particular conclusions (Darii and Ferio) can themselves be reduced. Thus Darii and Ferio can be *indirectly reduced* to Camestres and Cesare (Figure II) respectively and Camestres and Cesare can themselves be *directly reduced* to Celarent (Figure I). Cf. Aristotle, *Prior Analytics*, 29b.

fourth consists in displaying that each is logically equivalent to the first.

Again, those syllogisms can be shown to be equivalent which have one A premiss (major or minor) which is unconverted and, as the other premiss (major or minor), an I or an E proposition, converted or unconverted. Thus, as we can see, the members of the following three sets of moods are equivalent.

1.   I Celarent   II Cesare   II Camestres   IV Camenes
      No B is A = No A is B   All C is B = All C is B
      All C is B = All C is B   No A is B = No B is A
   ∴ No C is A = No C is A   =   No A is C = No A is C

2.   I Darii   III Datisi   III Disamis   IV Dimaris
      All B is A   = All B is A   Some B is C = Some C is B
      Some C is B = Some B is C   All B is A   = All B is A
   ∴ Some C is A = Some C is A   =   Some A is C = Some A is C

3.   III Felapton   IV Fesapo
                    No B is A   = No A is B
                    All B is C   = All B is C
                 ∴ Some C is not A = Some C is not A

In the above table the sign ' = ' is used to link logically equivalent propositional forms; A, B and C have been used instead of S, P and M. Which of the pair, A and C, is the major term and which the minor can be determined by the form of the conclusion in each case.

Thus we see that nine moods of the second, third and fourth figures are reducible to first figure moods (Ferio, Celarent and Darii) and a pair of moods of the third and fourth figure are equivalent. It remains to show how this latter pair of moods (Felapton and Fesapo), as well as Darapti (III) and Bramantip (IV), can be reduced to corresponding moods in I. These four moods are reduced by being shown to be not equivalent to but *implied by* the first figure moods, Ferio, Darii and Barbara. Thus

              III Darapti   I Darii
              All B is A   =   All B is A
              All B is C   implies   Some C is B
           ∴ Some C is A   =   Some C is A

The minor premiss 'All B is C' is converted *per accidens* to (and, hence, implies) 'Some C is B'. Since the conclusion 'Some C is A' follows from 'All B is A' and 'Some C is B' (which is a *weaker* premiss than 'All B is C'), it must also follow from the same major premiss, 'All B is A' together with 'All B is C' (which is a *stronger* premiss that 'Some C is B' and implies it). So much for the reduction of Darapti. In the same way Felapton and Fesapo are reduced to Ferio:

III Felapton	IV Fesapo	I Ferio
No B is A	= No A is B	= No B is A
All B is C	= All B is C implies	Some C is B
∴ Some C is not A	= Some C is not A	= Some C is not A

Finally Barbara implies Bramantip:

I Barbara	IV Bramantip
All B is A	All C is B
All C is B	All B is A
∴ All C is A implies	Some A is C

The conclusion of Bramantip is the converse *per accidens* of the conclusion of Barbara and is implied by it.

Indirect reduction: II Baroko and III Bokardo cannot be reduced by direct reduction to a first figure mood. We cannot arrive at a valid mood by converting the premisses since O is not convertible and I, the converse *per accidens* of A, cannot combine with O to constitute premisses of a valid mood. So, to prove these moods, Aristotle adopted a different procedure which is called reduction *ad impossibile*. Of this he says: "If all N is M and some X is not M, then some X is not N [II Baroko]; for if all X is N [contradictory of the conclusion] and all N is M [major premiss], then all X is M [contradictory of the minor premiss], but it was assumed that some X is not M [minor premiss]."[1] (The words in square brackets are not from Aristotle's text.) Aristotle is showing that the falsity of the conclusion of the original syllogism is incompatible with the truth of one of the premisses; he intends us to see that if those premisses are true, the original conclusion must follow from them. The procedure

[1] *Prior Analytics*, 24b.

constitutes a form of reduction because it is by reference to the mood Barbara, which is accepted as valid, that its validity is established. The interrelations of Baroko, Bokardo and Barbara may be shown as follows:

Baroko	All *B* is *A*	1.
	Some *C* is not *A*	2.
∴	Some *C* is not *B*	3.
Barbara	All *B* is *A* 1.	
	All *C* is *B*	contradictory of 3.
∴	All *C* is *A*	contradictory of 2.
Bokardo	Some *C* is not *A*	2.
	All *C* is *B*	contradictory of 3.
∴	Some *B* is not *A*	contradictory of 1.

A valid syllogism in Barbara is obtained by taking as premisses the contradictory of the conclusion of Baroko and its major premiss. If the contradictory of the conclusion together with the *minor* premiss of Baroko are taken as premisses, a syllogism in Bokardo results, the conclusion of which is the contradictory of the major premiss of Baroko. Bokardo itself can be indirectly reduced to Barbara by using the contradictory of its conclusion and its minor premiss as premisses to yield as a conclusion the contradictory of its major premiss.

The logic of indirect reduction becomes clearer when we recognise that it belongs not to the logic of terms but to the logic of propositions. Let 'If *P* and *Q*, then *R*' stand for the valid mood Barbara. Aristotle is in effect showing that 'If *P* and *Q*, then *R*' implies and is implied by 'If *P* and *Not-R*, then *Not-Q*' and that this implies and is implied by 'If *Q* and *Not-R*, then *Not-P*'. This logical law R. M. Eaton illustrates with an example: "If being healthy and young implies being optimistic, then being young and not optimistic implies not being healthy; and being healthy and not optimistic implies not being young." In fact Aristotle did not prove the law but outlined a procedure of reduction that exemplified it.[1]

[1] The law can be more neatly expressed in the notation of the propositional calculus, which will be explained in the next chapter:

$$((p \cdot q) \supset r) \equiv ((p \cdot \sim r) \supset \sim q) \equiv ((\sim r \cdot q) \supset \sim p)$$

This account of indirect reduction is largely derived from R. M. Eaton, *General Logic*, 1931, pp. 128–131.

Aristotle, of course, was not concerned to show simply that the three moods Barbara, Baroko and Bokardo stand or fall together but also that Baroko and Bokardo are *valid* moods. The form of the mood Barbara is 'If all *M* is *P* and all *S* is *M*, all *S* is *P*', and if we use propositional variables on this occasion to stand for the component propositional forms ('If *P* and *Q*, then *R*'), only the logical equivalence of the three moods can be displayed, not the validity of one or all of them. To display this we need the special notation of the logic of terms.

Traditional logic as a system

The doctrine of reduction makes it possible for us to regard traditional logic as the construction of a deductive system of inter-related laws. We may regard the moods of the first figure as un-demonstrated and indemonstrable axioms from which all the other valid moods can be deduced. Aristotle in fact (see note on p. 36) goes further and claims that only the two universal moods of the first figure, Barbara and Celarent, are necessary for this purpose. He does not, however, present the logic of the syllogism in the form in which other deductive systems, e.g. Euclidean geometry or the propositional calculus in Russell and Whitehead's *Principia Mathematica*, are usually presented. We are not given first defini-tions, then undemonstrated axioms, then a clear statement of the logical principles in accordance with which proofs will be carried out, and finally the deduction of derived laws (theorems) from the axioms in accordance with the given logical principles (or 'rules of in-ference'). Aristotle wrongly claimed that all proof was by syllogism. It may be that had he presented his arguments more in the manner of geometrical proofs he would have recognised that some of the laws in accordance with which he argues belong not to the logic of terms but to the logic of propositions (e.g. the laws 'if *p* and if *p* then *q*, then *q*' and 'if, if *p*, *q*, then if *not-q*, *not-p*,'), and that the laws of the square of opposition to which he appeals intuitively, without explicitly formulating them, and the laws of conversion, by which we infer immediately, belong to the logic of terms but are not syllogistic.

Recent logicians with the model of mathematical deductive systems before their minds are careful to distinguish between definitions, axioms and principles of inference and always make it clear which axioms they are adopting as starting-points and in accordance with what principles of inference demonstrations will be performed. Aristotle's presentation of logical notations is less systematic and more open to misinterpretation. It is largely on this account that disagreement is possible about what for Aristotle were the primitive axioms of the logic of the syllogism.

There are two passages in his work that have led some scholars to think that Aristotle held that only one axiom is needed, the so-called *Dictum de omni et nullo*. This is the medieval name for what was later considered the principle of the first figure. It has been formulated thus: "Whatever is affirmed or denied universally of something is also affirmed or denied of anything of which that thing is predicated." The two passages from which it is derived are the following: "That one term should be included in another as in a whole is the same as for the other to be predicated of all the first. And we may say that one term is predicated of all of another, whenever no instance of the subject can be found of which the other cannot be asserted: 'to be predicated of none' must be understood in the same way."[1] "When one thing is predicated of another all that which is predicable of the predicate will be predicable also of the subject."[2] But the first passage is intended merely as an explanation of the terminology that Aristotle proposes to use in his exposition, while the second occurs in a context in which there is no discussion of syllogisms at all. Aristotle nowhere explicitly claims that there is a single principle exemplified by syllogisms of the first figure.

What is more important is that Aristotle could not have thought that the *dictum*, however formulated, was an axiom from which the valid moods of the first figure could be deduced. As we have seen, he thought that all proof was syllogistic, so if the *dictum* were an axiom and we sought to prove from it the validity of Barbara, the proof, on his own account, would itself be a syllogism. Consider how such a proof would run:

> All arguments that satisfy the *dictum* are valid
> All syllogisms in Barbara satisfy the *dictum*
> ∴ All syllogisms in Barbara are valid

[1] *Prior Analytics*, 24b.
[2] *Categories*, 1a.

2*

The proof is itself of the form

$$\text{All } M \text{ is } P$$
$$\text{All } S \text{ is } M$$
$$\therefore \text{ All } S \text{ is } P$$

To adopt this procedure would be to purport to prove that syllogisms in Barbara were valid, by a syllogism in Barbara. So it is a precondition of the proof being possible that no proof is required. If 'If all M is P and all S is M, then all S is P' is not an axiom but a theorem to be derived, the proof required will need to be performed, not in accordance with the 'rule of inference', 'All M is P, All S is M $\therefore$ All S is P', but with some other principle or rule. But it is harmless to call the *dictum* the principle of universal syllogisms of the first figure if what is meant is that it is not the axiom guaranteeing the validity of Barbara and Celarent but a general statement in words of what is more usually expressed partly in words and partly in symbols, namely 'If all M is P and all S is M, then all S is P' and 'If no M is P and all S is M, then no S is P'.

If Aristotle had undertaken the task of presenting syllogistic logic as a deductive system he would, it seems, have taken the universal moods of the first figure as unproved axioms. It is perhaps idle to speculate what further axioms he would have added and whether he would have recognised that, in order to deduce from his axioms the other laws of syllogism, it is necessary to argue in accordance with other principles of inference than syllogistic principles. The Polish logician J. Łukasiewicz has shown how the logic of syllogism can be presented as such a system and what axioms and principles of inference it requires.[1]

Criticisms of traditional logic

The principal criticism that is raised against the Aristotelian-traditional logic is that it is an incomplete presentation of logical relations. Laws of the logic of propositions are either unrecognised or disguised as laws of the logic of terms. Although the logic of propositions was systematically investigated by Stoic logicians after the death of Aristotle, their discoveries had little effect on the development of traditional logic. It was only in the nineteenth

1 J. Łukasiewicz, *op. cit.*, chapters III and IV.

century that the importance of non-syllogistic logic began to be generally recognised. This general criticism is justified.

In the second place, criticism has been directed against traditional logic, on the grounds that, as an investigation of the logic of terms, it is incomplete and rests on a mistaken analysis of propositions. No adequate analysis is given, it is argued, of singular propositions, that is to say propositions about individuals, while the laws of conversion *per accidens* and some of the laws of the square of opposition presuppose an erroneous analysis of universal and particular propositions.

Singular propositions

Traditional logic represents singular and universal propositions as of the same form, 'All X is Y', a procedure which appears perverse but is intelligible. Just as in the phrase 'All men' the term 'men' is distributed, so we may say that the term 'Socrates', as the subject of a proposition, is also distributed, since it is used to refer to all that it can refer to, viz. the individual whose name is Socrates. In this respect 'All men are mortal' and 'Socrates is mortal' are analogous propositions in which mortality is predicated of all that to which the subject-term can apply. There are, it is true, significant differences between universal and singular propositions; singular propositions are not convertible, the individual cannot be predicated of anything, though propositions about individuals may be expressed in sentences of which the grammatical predicate is a proper name. Thus we may say "Wellington was the victor" or "The victor was Wellington", indifferently, to express a proposition of which 'Wellington' is the logical subject. Since, too, the individual cannot be predicated, a proper name cannot serve as middle-term except in the third figure, where it is subject in both premisses. Further, singular propositions have no contraries, and the contradictory of a singular proposition is not a particular proposition (i.e. no significant proposition is expressed by "No Socrates is wise" or "Some Socrates is not wise"). Thus the use of singular propositions as premisses or conclusions in syllogisms is limited.

In defence of the traditional notation, however, it may be said that where a singular term can occur, the proposition in which it occurs is logically indistinguishable from a universal affirmative proposition. If we were to define a universal proposition simply as one in which the subject-term is distributed, then a singular proposition is correctly classified as of 'All X is Y' form. By representing singular propositions as of the form 'All S is P', logicians marked the one formal characteristic which they share with universal propositions, in virtue of which they can be premisses and conclusions in syllogisms.

It is important to recognise that the formal analysis of propositions can be undertaken with different ends in view. On the one hand, we may be concerned for its own sake with the task of expounding their formal structure without reference to the logical relations in which propositions of different forms stand to one another. On the other hand, our analysis may have the more limited object of revealing only those formal features which are relevant for our understanding of logical relations. Criticism of formal analyses of propositions that logicians have given in the past has frequently been misdirected as a result of a failure to see the importance of this distinction. As we have seen, such a proposition as 'John is taller than Mary' can be the minor premiss of a syllogism. What is then logically relevant is that being taller than Mary is predicated of John, i.e. that it is of 'S is P' form. To say this is not to deny that a more detailed analysis can be given of it. The formula, 'All S is P', it will be argued, misrepresents the nature of universal propositions but it reflects the commonest way of expressing them in English and is thus useful in representing the logical relationships of premisses and conclusions in syllogisms.

Even where a formula (e.g. 'All S is P' for universal propositions) is both logically misleading and provides an incomplete analysis, its utility in representing the relationships of premisses and conclusions in syllogisms, and its close resemblance to common forms of expression in ordinary language, ensure its continued use in logical textbooks.

Laws of the square of opposition and conversion

The traditional doctrine is that A implies I, that both E and its converse imply O and that A can be converted to I *per accidens*. Unless these are valid forms of implication we must reject some of the accepted syllogistic moods and some of the laws of immediate inference. But are they valid?

It may be argued on the contrary that, for a proposition to hold universally, it is not necessary that either the subject-term or the predicate-term should be instantiated. To assert 'All offenders against this bye-law are liable to prosecution' is not to presuppose either that there are in fact offenders against the bye-law or that there are persons liable to prosecution. Even if it is the case (which may be denied) that the proposition 'No man is immortal' implies or presupposes that there are men, it does not imply that there are some things that are immortal. Thus the laws of the square of opposition and of conversion can apply only to propositions the subject-terms and predicate-terms of which are 'non-empty'. Yet it does not seem necessary for propositions to satisfy these conditions if they are to qualify as premisses or conclusions of valid syllogistic arguments. And this had led most logicians to the conclusion that the traditional scheme of logical relations must be abandoned on the grounds that A does not imply I, that A is not convertible *per accidens*, that neither E nor its converse implies O. Thereby all the traditionally accepted moods of the syllogism which have universal premisses and particular conclusions are rejected as invalid; namely AAI and EAO in Figure I, EAO and AEO in Figure II, AEO, AAI and EAO in Figure III, and AAI and EAO in Figure IV.

There are two principal ways in which these radical criticisms of the traditional logic are met:

1. We may grant that the laws of traditional logic hold only between propositions which satisfy the existential presuppositions which we have noticed. The objection to adopting this line of defence is that it amounts to an admission that the system provides no analysis of the logical relations of the many propositions that do *not* carry these existential commitments. It is unlikely that its supporters would be prepared to acquiesce in a defence according to which its scope was so drastically limited.

2. A different line of defence is offered by Łukasiewicz. He argues thus: Aristotle did not introduce into his logic singular or empty terms, only universal terms, such as 'man' and 'animal', and even these terms belong only to the application of the system, not to the system itself. In the system we have only expressions involving

variables ('*B* belongs to all *A*' etc.) and their negations; and two of these expressions are undefined primitive terms: they have only those properties which are stated by the axioms. The syllogistic of Aristotle (he maintains) is a theory neither of classes nor of predicates; it exists apart from other deductive systems, having its own axioms and its own problems.[1]

The differences between these two points of view may not be obvious, but they are important and it will be well to emphasise them. Whereas, according to the first, traditional logic is an attempt, though a very incomplete one, to present correctly the structure of argument and of the propositions of which arguments are composed, the second point of view represents Aristotle's intention as being that of constructing a consistent system of formal relations between formulae rather than an analysis of what laymen recognise as propositions and valid arguments. The relation of such formulae as 'All *A* is *B*' to the universal propositions of ordinary discourse is not, on this view, a matter of central importance to Aristotle, although we are told that, when the system is applied, we are entitled to substitute general, non-empty terms for *A* and *B* in the formulae. If there were no propositions of ordinary discourse of which Aristotle's formulae provide an adequate analysis, no defect in the system would thereby be revealed. It is by no means clear that Aristotle would have welcomed this second line of defence. In these points of view we may see two different directions in which logicians may pursue their investigations. The first leads to closer investigation of the forms and the language of the arguments of everyday life, the second to the construction of ordered systems of relations which generate their own specialised problems.

Traditional logic fails to provide a complete and satisfactory formal analysis of propositions and their logical relations. In later chapters we shall consider the defects that have been revealed and see to what extent modern logic has succeeded in providing an analysis that is free of them.

[1] J. Łukasiewicz, *op. cit.*, p. 130.

3

THE LOGIC OF PROPOSITIONS

Traditional logic recognised as valid two forms of hypothetical argument that belong not to the logic of terms but to the logic of propositions. These were called by medieval logicians the *modus ponens* and the *modus tollens*.

The form of the former is

$$\text{If } p, \text{ then } q$$
$$p$$
$$\therefore q$$

and of the latter

$$\text{If } p, \text{ then } q$$
$$\text{not } q$$
$$\therefore \text{ not } p$$

In addition it recognised two forms of disjunctive argument

$$\text{Either } p \text{ or } q$$
$$p$$
$$\therefore \text{ not } q$$

and

$$\text{Either } p \text{ or } q$$
$$\text{not } q$$
$$\therefore p$$

These kinds of inference depend on the formal relation of antecedent to consequent and that of disjunction (between propositions), not on the *internal* structure of the component propositions. But the fact that, for example, the internal structure of the antecedent and of the consequent in an argument of the *modus ponens* form is irrelevant to its validity was not recognised by traditional logicians, though it had been noticed by Stoic logicians shortly after the death of Aristotle. Arguments of this form were symbolized in the notation of the logic of terms as

$$\text{If } A \text{ is } B, C \text{ is } D$$
$$A \text{ is } B$$
$$\therefore \ C \text{ is } D$$

and were described as hypothetical syllogisms. In R. M. Eaton's words, "by masking these relationships between propositions behind the general subject-predicate analysis and by squeezing them into the syllogistic forms which are based on this analysis, traditional logicians concealed from themselves the need for a more general treatment of logic that would include the logic of elementary propositions as well as that of terms."[1] In fact they failed to see altogether that the logic of elementary propositions was a branch of logic that called for investigation.

The logic of propositions consists of those laws of logical necessity which hold between propositions *whatever their internal structure may be*. These laws can be presented in a logical vocabulary which consists simply of signs for unanalysed propositions, for negation, for the conjunction and disjunction of propositions and for the relation of antecedent and consequent. As we have seen, the law that is exemplified by the proposition that it is logically impossible for 'Tom is Australian' and 'Tom is not Australian' both to be true is one of these laws. In order to present them unambiguously and succinctly, a special notation has been invented in which there are special signs for negation, conjunction, disjunction and the antecedent-consequent relation and for other relations definable in terms of them, and in which letters of the alphabet stand for unanalysed or uncompounded propositions. If we use these special signs we commit ourselves to the rules that govern their use in the system of propositional logic which is called the 'calculus of propositions'. The calculus of propositions, it is important to recognise, provides us with one, but not necessarily the only possible, systematic presentation of the laws of propositional logic. But it is this system which will now be briefly expounded.

[1] R. M. Eaton, *op. cit.*, p. 157, slightly paraphrased.

The propositional calculus

The letters *p, q, r* etc. are *proposition-variables*; that is to say, they can stand for any propositions whatsoever.

The special signs, which are called *constants*, are ' $\sim$ ', ' $\cdot$ ', ' $\vee$ ', ' $\supset$ ', ' $\equiv$ ', ' $/$ '. No one of these can be used in isolation but only in conjunction with propositions or proposition-variables.

' $\sim$ ' is the sign for negation and always precedes a proposition or proposition-variable.

' $\cdot$ ', the sign for conjunction, and ' $\vee$ ', the sign for disjunction, link propositions or proposition-variables.

' $\supset$ ', called the 'material-implication' sign, links propositions or proposition-variables. *Very roughly*, it represents the relation between antecedent and consequent.

' $\equiv$ ', the 'material-equivalence' sign, links propositions or proposition-variables which are either both true or both false; of which, to put it differently, the *truth-values* are the same.

' $/$ ', the 'stroke-function' or 'stroke-sign', is also a linking sign and signifies that not both of the propositions linked are true.

Every complete formula, constructed according to the rules of the system, represents a proposition or the form of a proposition.[1] Every proposition, whether simple or compound, is either true or false. We define the constants by stating the conditions under which compound propositions involving those constants are true or false. Thus we define ' $\sim$ ' when we say that ' $\sim p$ ' is true if ' p ' is false and false if ' p ' is true. Similarly, we define ' $\cdot$ ' when we say that ' $p \cdot q$ ' is true if both ' p ' and ' q ' are true, false if either ' p ' or ' q ' or both ' p ' and ' q ' are false. ' $p \vee q$ ' is true if ' p ' is true or ' q ' is true or both ' p ' and ' q ' are true. ' $p \supset q$ ' is true if ' p ' and ' q ' are both true or both false or if ' p ' is false and ' q ' is true; it is false only if ' p ' is true and ' q ' is false. ' $p \equiv q$ ' is true if ' p ' and ' q ' are either both false or both true. ' p/q ' is true if either ' p ' or ' q ' is false or if both are false; it is false if both ' p ' and ' q ' are true.

The constants are not all primitive and independent but to a certain degree interdefinable. Thus ' $p \cdot q$ ' can be defined as

[1] On this point, see p. 54. In this chapter I have compressed the exposition of the calculus by ignoring typographically the difference between sentence-forms and proposition-forms. Thus, for example, ' $\sim p$ ' can serve to present, in one context, a sentence-form, of which ' $\sim$ ' and ' p ' are component signs, and, in another context, the form of a negative proposition.

' $\sim(\sim p \vee \sim q)$ '.[1] In the same way, in English, we could dispense with 'and' if we had a vocabulary that included 'or' and 'not', and replace "Jack fell down and Jill came tumbling after", cumbersomely, by "It is not the case that either Jack did not fall down or Jill did not come tumbling after". The constants ' $\supset$ ' and ' $\equiv$ ' can be defined in terms of ' $\cdot$ ' and ' $\sim$ ' or of 'v' and ' $\sim$ ', while, as we have seen, formulae employing ' $\cdot$ ' and ' $\sim$ ' can be replaced by others employing 'v' and ' $\sim$ ' (and *vice versa*). Thus just as ' $p \cdot q$ ' can be defined as ' $\sim(\sim p \vee \sim q)$ ', so ' $p \vee q$ ' can be defined as ' $\sim(\sim p \cdot \sim q)$ '. ' $p \supset q$ ' can be replaced either by ' $\sim p \vee q$ ' or by ' $\sim(p \cdot \sim q)$ ', since, as we have seen, a proposition of the form ' $p \supset q$ ' is false only if ' p ' is true and ' q ' false (for all other truth-values of ' p ' and ' q ', ' $p \supset q$ ' is true) and the same truth-conditions hold for ' $\sim p \vee q$ ' and for ' $\sim(p \cdot \sim q)$ '. In the same way, ' $p \equiv q$ ' may be replaced by ' $(p \supset q) \cdot (q \supset p)$ '.

These replacements of a formula, in which one set of constants is used, by another formula, in which others are used, appear more intelligible to some if the constants are replaced by equivalent (or nearly equivalent) conjunctions in English. For this purpose ' $\sim$ ' may be read as or replaced by 'not', 'v' by 'or', ' $\cdot$ ' by 'and', ' $\supset$ ' by 'if' (whereby ' $p \supset q$ ' is read as 'if p, q '), ' $\equiv$ ' by 'if and only if'. Thus we can see that to equate definitionally ' $p \supset q$ ' with ' $\sim p \vee q$ ' or ' $\sim(p \cdot \sim q)$ ' is to equate in meaning 'if p, q ' with 'either not-p or q ' or 'not both p and not-q ' (or, more idiomatically 'not p without q '). To take a particular case, we treat as synonymous: "If it is raining the sun is concealed", "Either it is not raining or the sun is concealed", "It is not raining without the sun being concealed".

The interdefinability of the constants of the calculus makes it possible for their number to be reduced to two— ' $\sim$ ' and 'v'; ' $\sim$ ' and ' $\cdot$ '; or ' $\sim$ and $\supset$ '—or, if the stroke-function is admitted, by it alone.[2]

---

[1] As I do not intend to give more than a brief review of the calculus I shall not give a detailed exposition of it. The function of brackets can be readily grasped by anyone who has studied elementary algebra. In this case it is to make it clear that the part of the formula within brackets is negatived as a whole by the preceding ' $\sim$ '. In ' $\sim(\sim p \vee \sim q)$ ', ' $(\sim p \vee \sim q)$ ' is the *scope* of the first ' $\sim$ '. Similarly, by ' $(p \vee q) \vee r$ ' we express the disjunction of ' $p \vee q$ ' as a whole with ' r '; by ' $p \vee (q \vee r)$ ' we express the disjunction of ' p ' with ' $q \vee r$ ' as a whole.

[2] Since ' p/q ' is true if at least one of the pair ' p ' and ' q ' is false, ' p/q ' is equivalent to ' $\sim(p \cdot q)$ ' or to ' $\sim p \vee \sim q$ '. If we use the stroke-function as sole

Thus we can express all the relations between propositions on which the logic of propositions depends, namely negation, conjunction, disjunction, material implication and material equivalence, by means of two constants only. These (whether ' $\sim$ ' and ' $\cdot$ ', ' $\sim$ ' and 'v', or ' $\sim$ ' and ' $\supset$ ') may be regarded as signs for primitive and undefined concepts. But, just as it would be inconvenient to reduce the logical connections of ordinary language to 'and' and 'not', or 'or' and 'not', so it is usually considered inconvenient to reduce the constants of the calculus to two, and formulae employing the other constants which have been listed (apart from the stroke-function) are usually introduced as definitional abbreviations of formulae in which only the basic pair are used. Definitions are introduced thus:[1]

$$P \supset Q = \sim(P \cdot \sim Q) \qquad \text{Df.}$$
$$P \vee Q = \sim(\sim P \cdot \sim Q) \qquad \text{Df.}$$

What determines the truth of compound propositions, that is to say propositions which are negated or involve disjunction, conjunction, material implication or material equivalence, is the truth or falsity of the uncompounded propositions from which they are constructed. Thus '$p \cdot q$' is true if 'p' is true and 'q' is true; '$p \supset q$' is false if and only if 'p' is true and 'q' is false. There is nothing that should surprise us about this. 'Jack fell down and Jill came tumbling after' is a true compound proposition if it is true both that Jack fell down and that Jill came tumbling after. It is clear, then, that we could go on indefinitely constructing formulae for compound propositions which would be *contingently* true or false according as their component propositions were true or false. But there are some

constant, 'p/p', replaces ' $\sim p$', '$(p/q)/(p/q)$' replaces '$p \cdot q$', '$(p/p)/(q/q)$' replaces '$p \vee q$', '$p/(q/q)$' replaces '$p \supset q$'. That the truth-values of both members of each of these pairs of formulae is the same can be checked by truth-tables (see p. 54). We shall not use the stroke-function in later examples. The gain in respect of notational economy is outweighed, at least at first, by the loss in immediate intelligibility in the resulting formulae.

[1] The sign ' $= \ldots$ Df' is not a constant of the propositional calculus and is therefore not used in formulae expressing logical laws. It is only used to explain the interpretation of the symbols used in expressing logical laws. The reason for using capital letters, 'P', 'Q', 'R' etc., in definitions and in the expression of the rules of the calculus, instead of the variables 'p', 'q', 'r' etc., is the wish to mark off definitions and rules from the laws of the system and to indicate that definitions and rules apply with full generality to all formulae of the calculus.

formulae which will always yield true propositions and others that will always yield false ones, whatever propositions we substitute for the component '*p*'s' and '*q*'s' and '*r*'s'. Thus whatever proposition we substitute for '*p*' in ' $\sim(p \cdot \sim p)$ ', a true compound proposition will result, and whatever we substitute for '*p*' in '*p* $\cdot \sim p$' a false proposition will result. Thus we can distinguish three kinds of formulae: 1. Contingent, such as '*p* $\supset q$' which can yield a true or a false compound proposition. 2. Logically true, logically necessary, such as '*p* $\vee \sim p$'; such formulae express logical laws. 3. Logically false, logically impossible, such as '*p* $\cdot \sim p$'.

Truth-tables

There is a simple method of establishing whether formulae are contingent, logically necessary or logically impossible and whether sets of formulae are or are not equivalent. This is the truth-table method and it can most easily be explained by giving examples of its use. The following is the truth-table for the formula '*p* $\supset q$':

	p	q	$p \supset q$
1.	T	T	T
2.	T	F	F
3.	F	T	T
4.	F	F	T

On the top line at the right is printed the formula under consideration. To its left are listed in separate columns its component propositional variables and below them four combinations of T (True) and F (False) which exhaust the possible combinations of true and false for those components. To the right of these columns and below the constant are listed the corresponding truth-values (i.e. T or F) of the formula as a whole, for all the possible combinations of T and F for the components. We can now read off the possible truth-values of the formulae, horizontally and line by line: "If *p* is true and *q* is true, then *p* $\supset q$ is true; if *p* is true and *q* is false, then *p* $\supset q$ is false; if *p* is false and *q* is true, then *p* $\supset q$ is true; if *p* is false and *q* is false, then *p* $\supset q$ is true." This table can be interpreted as laying down the 'truth-conditions' of the formula '*p* $\supset q$' and thereby stating the rules for the use of the sign ' $\supset$ '.

Next let us consider a case where the rules for the use of the constant ' ⊃ ' are assumed and our task is to decide on the truth-conditions of a formula, in the light of knowledge of those rules.

	p	q	r	$[(p{\supset}q) \cdot (q{\supset}r)]$			$\supset(p{\supset}r)$	
1.	T	T	T	T	T	T	T	T
2.	T	T	F	T	F	F	T	F
3.	T	F	T	F	F	T	T	T
4.	T	F	F	F	F	T	T	F
5.	F	T	T	T	T	T	T	T
6.	F	T	F	T	F	F	T	T
7.	F	F	T	T	T	T	T	T
8.	F	F	F	T	T	T	T	T
				(1)	(4)	(2)	(5)	(3)

The numbers below the columns of T's and F's give the order in which the truth-values of the parts of the formula, for all truth-values of the constituent elementary propositions, are calculated.

Thus the constants in columns (1) (2) and (3), which are ' ⊃ ' in every case, have the most restricted scope; the scope of ' · ' (column (4)) is wider (it links '$(p{\supset}q)$' and '$(q{\supset}r)$'), while the scope of ' ⊃ ' in column (5), called the *main constant*, is widest of all. Brackets indicate both which elements are to be taken together and in what order they are to be taken. The main constant may be compared to the main verb of a compound sentence, the others to the verbs in subordinate clauses. The truth-values in column (4) are determined by the truth-values in columns (1) and (2), while those of column (5), which are the truth-values of the formula as a whole, are determined by those of columns (4) and (3). As we have already said, the truth value of a formula or part of a formula is determined by the truth or falsity of the component elementary propositional forms, in accordance with the rules for its constant. In this truth-table it will be seen that column (5) consists of an unbroken series of T's. Thus for all possible combinations of truth-values for 'p', 'q', and 'r', the formula expresses a proposition that is true. '$[(p{\supset}q) \cdot (q{\supset}r)]{\supset}(p{\supset}r)$' is therefore logically true or a logical law. Where the column under the main constant in a truth-table consists of mixed

T's and F's the formula is contingent; where it consists of a series of F's it is logically false.

A third example will show how we may by truth-tables display the equivalence of formulae.

p	q	$p \supset q$	$\sim p \vee q$
T	T	T	T
T	F	F	F
F	T	T	T
F	F	T	T

For all truth-values of 'p' and 'q', where '$p \supset q$' is true, '$\sim p \vee q$' is true; where '$p \supset q$' is false, '$\sim p \vee q$' is false. Thus they are logically equivalent formulae and each can be substituted for the other with no change in truth-value.

Propositional forms

A word is called for at this stage about the *status* of the formulae of the calculus of propositions. '$p \supset q$' is not itself a proposition but a propositional form. It is neither true nor false but is a form which both true and false propositions may take. By contrast '$p \vee \sim p$' can be interpreted either as a propositional form or as a logical law. It is a propositional form in that it may be exemplified, for example, by 'Either Tom is Australian or Tom is not Australian'. At the same time it might be intended as the (incomplete) formulation of a law, to be read as 'For any proposition whatsoever, whether true or false, either it is true or it is not true' or 'Every proposition is either true or false'.[1] Similarly, it is reasonable to ascribe a dual status to

[1] For the unambiguous formulation of logical laws we need a sign for 'universal quantification'. Thus the law of excluded middle (that necessarily every proposition is either true or false) would be expressed as '$(p)(p \vee \sim p)$', where '(p)' is to be read as 'Whatever proposition p may be', and is known technically as a 'universal quantifier'. If a formula expresses a logical law, we should always understand its component propositional variables as universally quantified. So, as the expression of a law, '$[(p \supset q) \cdot (q \supset r)] \supset (p \supset r)$' is an abbreviation for '$(p)(q)(r)\{[(p \supset q) \cdot (q \supset r)] \supset (p \supset r)\}$'. But quantifiers may be (and commonly are) omitted when it is clear from the context that a formula is to be understood as expressing a law.

such formulae as '$p \cdot \sim p$' and to describe them either as propositional forms or as logical impossibilities.[1]

The system

We can now see how, without or—more easily—with the aid of truth-tables, it is possible to list the formulae of the calculus of propositions under different headings. Under one we can set logical laws, under another logical impossibilities, under a third contingent formulae. Further, we can display the logical relationships which hold between formulae, that one formula is consistent or inconsistent with or equivalent to another, and so on. But logicians have not been satisfied with such an unsystematic procedure. Instead they have undertaken the much more considerable task of showing that the laws of propositional logic are interdependent and constitute a completely intelligible deductive system of logic. The most influential of pioneers in this undertaking were Whitehead and Russell, and it is the procedure which they followed which we shall briefly consider.

First, certain ideas or concepts are accepted as primitive and undefined; next, other ideas or concepts are defined in terms of them, written or printed signs being invented for expressing them. Thereafter certain propositions are laid down as primitive laws or axioms. These serve as premisses from which are deduced (or 'derived') all the remaining laws of the logic of propositions. These are called theorems and are analogous to the theorems of geometry. The deduction of theorems from the axioms of the system is carried through in accordance with a limited number of principles of inference.

In the system of *Principia Mathematica*[2] the following concepts are treated as primitive:

1. That of the proposition, represented by the letters 'p', 'q', 'r' etc;
2. That of inclusive disjunction, represented by ' $\vee$ ', whereby a proposition of the form '$p \vee q$' is true if either 'p' or 'q' or both 'p' and 'q' are true;
3. That of propositional negation, represented by ' $\sim$ '.

[1] But see the end of this chapter.
[2] 1st ed., 1903.

Three constants are introduced by definition:

$$P \supset Q = \sim P \vee Q \quad \text{Df.}$$
$$P \cdot Q = \sim (\sim P \vee \sim Q) \quad \text{Df.}$$
$$P \equiv Q = (P \supset Q) \cdot (Q \supset P) \quad \text{Df.}$$

Five primitive laws are selected:

1. $(p \vee p) \supset p$
2. $q \supset (p \vee q)$
3. $(p \vee q) \supset (q \vee p)$
4. $(p \vee (q \vee r)) \supset (q \vee (p \vee r))$
5. $(q \supset r) \supset ((p \vee q) \supset (p \vee r))$

Derivation of the other laws of the propositional calculus is performed in accordance with three operational rules.

1. The *rule of substitution on variables:* whereby any propositional variable in a logically true formula may be uniformly replaced by any other 'truth-functional' formula, that is to say by any formula constructed out of the symbols of the calculus that can stand for a true or false proposition. Thus, if '$p \supset p$' is a law, the substitution of '$p \vee q$' for 'p' throughout yields a law '$(p \vee q) \supset (p \vee q)$'.

2. The *rule of substitution by definition:* whereby in a logically true formula we may substitute for any formula another formula equivalent to it according to the definitions of the constants in the system. Thus if '$P \cdot Q = \sim (\sim P \vee \sim Q)$ Df.' for '$p \cdot q \supset q \cdot p$' we may substitute '$\sim (\sim p \vee \sim q) \supset \sim (\sim q \vee \sim p)$'.

3. The *rule of inference*, which is the principle of *modus ponens*, whereby if 'P' and '$P \supset Q$' are both laws, we may deduce 'Q' as a law.

It is not suggested that only from the first laws listed, and not from any other alternative set of laws, can the remaining laws of the logic of propositions be derived, or that only the constants, ' $\sim$ ' and '$\vee$', can be accepted as primitive. It is recognised that three axioms can be substituted for the five of *Principia Mathematica*, and some logicians have accepted ' $\sim$ ' and ' $\cdot$ ', or ' $\sim$ ' and ' $\supset$ ', or the stroke-function as primitive.

To have selected a handful of axioms which were necessary, independent and consistent, and from which the remaining laws of propositional logic could be rigorously deduced, was an achievement of the first magnitude in the history of logic. Together with the construction of the proofs of the theorems, it is an undertaking comparable in originality and imaginative insight with the systematisation of Euclidean geometry. This is a fact that we may easily fail to recognise, since to *follow through* the proofs, after they have been constructed, demands of the student no more than that he should master the notation and recognise, step by step, the logical conclusiveness of the argument. To do this calls for neither originality nor imagination.

Yet it is not my intention here to illustrate the procedure of proof adopted. We should notice in passing that the traditional laws of thought, represented in the calculus by '$p \supset p$' (the Law of Identity), '$\sim (p \cdot \sim p)$' (the Law of Non-contradiction), '$p \vee \sim p$' (the Law of Excluded Middle), are not included in the axioms of the system. Though the five selected are necessary and self-evident, they are no more obvious than many other laws. What determined their selection was the fact that from them the rest could be derived. It was not relevant to the purpose of the constructors of the system that other laws may seem, from a 'common-sense point of view', more fundamental or important.

Logic and the calculus

It is proper to ask what entitles us to call this system which we have been considering a *logical* system. To this the answer is simple. The axioms which serve as premisses are necessary laws of logic, and the theorems derived from them follow in accordance with other necessary logical laws or principles. The axioms are not arbitrarily selected or prescribed; that is to say, they do not hold good because a logical innovator has laid them down. They are not *rules* in the sense of the word 'rules' in which we speak of 'rules of a game'. It makes no sense to speak of such rules as necessary or true; they hold because the inventor of the game has decided that they *shall* hold. The axioms, then, of the calculus of propositions are undemonstrated, necessary truths. If it be asked how we know that they are necessary, we are driven in the end to answer that they are self-evident; that is to say we are driven to appeal to a psychological rather than a logical fact, that we intuitively recognise them to be true.[1]

As we have had occasion to notice before, a prerequisite of the study of logic is the capacity to distinguish the logically true from the logically false, the valid from the invalid. But the vocabulary which we use in speaking about the calculus of propositions may easily mislead us into misunderstanding its nature, in particular the application of the word 'rules' to the operational procedures in accordance with which the theorems are proved. They are rules in so far as they prescribe the ways within the system in which demonstrations are to be carried out. But they are only prescribable because they are, independently of any logician's prescription, valid forms of inference. If two expressions are, from a logical point of view, synonymous, then it is valid to substitute one for the other; the rule that permits uniform substitution on variables can only be a rule because it expresses a *true* principle of logic. The rule that within the system we are permitted to move from premisses to conclusion by *modus ponens* does not command us to make inferences of this kind, rather it forbids us to include in our proofs inferences of other kinds.

Strictly there can be no such thing as a 'rule of inference'. There can only be rules for doing things that we can do at will or to order, and we do not infer at will or to order. To infer is not to 'make a move' but to recognise that an implication holds; it is not, in an active sense, for me to *do* anything at all but rather a case of something happening to me. A policeman can be ordered to scrutinise all visitors to a government office; he cannot be ordered to *recognise* them. We can no more decide to infer from propositions which we believe to be true that another proposition is true, than the policeman can decide to recognise every third visitor to his office. To command another to infer from the fact that all men are mortal and all Greeks are men that all Greeks are mortal would be to misuse language or to betray a radical misunderstanding of the nature of thinking. Either I 'see' (or 'it strikes me') that the consequence follows or I fail to see it. But if I were to fail to see that a consequence followed, I could not make good the defect by *deciding* to see that it did. Thus if I infer in accordance with the principle of *modus ponens*, it is because it is a valid principle. I can only be required to

[1] But this is not the whole story, as I shall attempt to show in ch. 7.

infer in accordance with it in the sense that I can be required, in a given logical system, not to *count* as proofs demonstrations in accordance with other valid logical principles.

Proof always presupposes the validity of logical principles. In proving, we must appeal to the capacity of our hearers or readers to distinguish between valid and invalid arguments. We may indeed construct deductive systems the premisses of which are arbitrary postulates with no claim to truth or logical necessity, but which hold only because it is laid down that they shall hold; but when we develop such systems and deduce theorems from those postulates, the principles in accordance with which we carry out our derivations cannot themselves have the status of arbitrary rules of procedure. They, by contrast with the premisses of the system, must be valid principles of logic. As I have said, the propositional calculus is not such a system. In being a *logical* system, the premisses from which it starts are necessary logical principles and therefore of the same status as the principles in accordance with which theorems are deduced. In fact all the laws of the system, whether primitive or derived, are laws of valid inference. The calculus of propositions presents consistently the logic of propositions; and it shows how, in recognising certain forms of propositions as logical laws, we are committed, in accordance with those laws, to other logical laws, which can indeed be recognised independently.

The interpretation of the constants

If we are to accept the claim that the calculus provides us with a correct analysis of propositional logic, we must be satisfied that the constants of the system adequately represent the formal properties of negative and compound propositions and thereby their possible logical relations. Do the definitions of the constants justify us in interpreting '$\sim p$' as 'not-p', '$p \cdot q$' as 'p and q', '$p \vee q$' as 'p or q', '$p \supset q$' as 'if p, q'?

'$\sim$' raises no difficulties as the sign for propositional negation, used in conjunction with either propositions, as '$\sim$(Tom is Australian)', or propositional forms. It may be read as 'not'.

'$\cdot$', the sign used to conjoin propositions or propositional forms, appears at first sight to differ in function from the English word 'and'. In the calculus, the order of conjoined propositions is irrelevant, and '$p \cdot q$' is materially equivalent to '$q \cdot p$'. But propositions linked by 'and' seem sometimes to change in meaning when reversed. "John got down to work and passed the examination" is not idiomatically interchangeable with "John passed the examination and got down to work". But this apparent disparity does not reveal any inadequacy in the calculus. In the English sentence quoted, 'and' is equivalent to 'and afterwards' or 'and in consequence'. Thus, when we utter it, what we are asserting is, first, that John got down to work and, second, that, after or as a result of getting down to work, he passed the examination. Thus the second proposition is not, after all, the same proposition as 'John got down to work · John passed the examination'. The lesson that we should draw is that whereas ' · ' is the sign for bare conjunction, 'and', in English, is something used idiomatically to convey more than bare conjunction.

It is to be noticed that the constant ' · ' serves not only for 'and' but also for 'but' and 'although'. This is a strength and not a weakness of the notation. In employing a single constant to express conjunction, however it may be expressed in natural languages, the calculus sifts the logically relevant from the logically irrelevant. 'But' differs from 'and' in that it not only conjoins propositions but also reveals the attitude of the speaker (or the attitude that the speaker anticipates in his audience) to the propositions asserted. Whichever word he selects, it is the same proposition that is asserted, and it is with the forms of propositions, not with our *attitude* to propositions, that logic is concerned. What determines a man to say "She is poor but she is honest," rather than "She is poor and she is honest", is a problem for psychology or sociology. It is of no logical interest.

The constant ' v ' signifies inclusive and not exclusive disjunction; that is to say, a proposition of the form '$p \lor q$' is true not only if one of the disjuncts is true but also if both are, whereas, in traditional logic, disjunctive connections are taken to *exclude* the truth of both disjuncts. On either interpretation the falsity of both disjuncts is excluded. In the calculus the force of exclusive disjunction can be made explicitly by expressions of the form '$(p \lor q) \cdot \sim (p \cdot q)$'. It seems that conventional usage alone determines whether, in any given language, disjunctions are to be interpreted as inclusive or exclusive. But it is more convenient in a calculus to operate with a connective that is inclusive. So long as the rules for 'v' are understood, it may without confusion be read as 'or'.

The constant '⊃' raises greater difficulties; and the claim that it accurately represents the relation between antecedent and consequent in a hypothetical proposition calls for longer discussion than problems raised by the other constants. Propositions of the form '$p \supset q$' are true if 'p' is true and 'q' is true, if 'p' is false and 'q' is true or false, false only if 'p' is true and 'q' is false. If the same truth-conditions hold for hypothetical propositions, then the following sentences will express true hypotheticals:

1. 'If Cromwell died in 1658, Oxford is a university city'
2. 'If Cromwell died in 1660, Oxford is a university city'
3. 'If Cromwell died in 1660, Oxford is the capital of Spain'

For in 1., both antecedent and consequent are true; in 2., the antecedent is false and the consequent true; and in 3., both the antecedent and the consequent are false. Does the fact that propositions such as these are not asserted in ordinary discourse and that, even if they did occur, we should not know whether to call them true or false, discredit the claim that '⊃' represents 'if'?

The hypothetical propositions which we have occasion to assert are *conditional* propositions, the antecedent giving the conditions under which the consequent is realised.[1] To assert 'If it rains, the match will be cancelled' is to state a condition under which the match will be cancelled. Thus, for a hypothetical proposition to be plausible, it is usually necessary that we should see the realisation of the antecedent as relevant to the realisation of the consequent. This relevance is lacking in 1., 2., and 3. The date of Cromwell's death has no bearing on the truth of the three consequents.

Let us see if we can establish in what way antecedents are relevant to consequences. It has often been assumed that the relationship is one of implication. The antecedent of the proposition, 'If no communists are M.P.s, no M.P.s are communists', entails the consequent, as does the antecedent of 'If John is a bachelor, he is unmarried'. But it is one of the achievements of the pioneers of

[1] But see note on p. 63.

propositional logic to have recognised that, although it is natural to express implications in the hypothetical form, no such relation as that of implication need hold between antecedent and consequent. The falling of rain does not *imply*, but is causally related to, the cancellation of a cricket match. But because implying and implied propositions are commonly linked hypothetically, it is an easy mistake to assume that the function of 'if', as such, is to express a logical relation. There is in fact no one sort of relevance of proposition to proposition that needs to exist, if they are to be linked hypothetically. But the *minimum* condition that must be satisfied, if a hypothetical proposition is to be true, is that it is not the case that the antecedent is true and the consequent false. It is a little paradoxical, however, that this minimal relationship should be called 'material implication'. It is misleading to use the word 'implication', however qualified, to name a relation which holds between 'p' and 'q', whether or not 'p' implies 'q', in any ordinary sense, provided only that it is not the case that 'p' is true and 'q' false.

The doctrine implicit in the calculus is that the only fact about true hypothetical propositions that is relevant to the logical relations in which they may stand is, so far as the logic of elementary propositions is concerned, that it is not the case that their antecedents are true and their consequents false. It is not denied that the fact that in a given case this condition is satisfied may not be an adequate reason for linking propositions hypothetically, and the logician is no more inclined than the layman to assert such contingent hypotheticals as 'If Cromwell died in 1658, Oxford is a university city'. He, of course, would agree that one would not, in practice, make such an assertion, unless one thought of the truth of the antecedent as being in some way a condition under which the consequent would be true. The calculus is not concerned with the analysis of the forms of contingent hypothetical propositions for its own sake, but only in that they can occur as components of logical laws. The law '$(p \supset q) \supset (\sim q \supset \sim p)$' has, as components, the contingent formulae '$p \supset q$' and '$\sim q \supset \sim p$'. What propositions could be linked as 'p' and 'q', to form a significant hypothetical proposition of the form '$p \supset q$', is a question which the logician need not ask or answer. What he is concerned to show is that, if a significant proposition is substituted for '$p \supset q$', it will entail a proposition of the form ' $\sim q \supset \sim p$ '. 'If it is the case that, if Cromwell died in 1658, Oxford is a university city, then it follows that, if Oxford is not a university city, Cromwell did not die in 1658' is a significant proposition in spite of the fact that the hypothetical propositions on which it is constructed (and which are *not* asserted as true) are not propositions that we should ever have occasion to utter. Thus, the claim implicit in the calculus is that it is logically irrelevant what, if any, relation of relevance holds between the antecedents and the consequents of contingent hypothetical propositions.

Yet, even if we admit the strength of this claim, we may still consider that '$p \supset q$' is importantly different in meaning from 'if p, q'. 'If it rains, the match will be cancelled' is inconsistent with 'If it rains, the match will not be cancelled'; one proposition is, in ordinary English, the 'contrary' of the other. But, in the calculus, '$p \supset q$' and '$p \supset \sim q$' represent the forms of propositions which can both be true together, while ' $\sim p \supset (p \supset q)$' and ' $\sim p \supset (p \supset \sim q)$' are both logically true.

Let us see how this disparity arises. When we say something of the form, 'if p, q', we assert what occurs in a given condition, and our assertion is falsified if, though the condition is satisfied, the consequent is not realised.[1] What then do we say if the condition is not satisfied? If 'if p, q' had the same force as '$p \supset q$', we should say that the original proposition was verified, since propositions of the form '$p \supset q$' are true if 'p' is false. But this is not the answer that we should give. Our original proposition—and let us say that it was 'If it rains, the match will be cancelled'—does not assert what will happen if it does *not* rain, only what will happen if it does rain. The proposition neither provides nor purports to provide any information about what would be the case if the condition were not realised. Thus, in the case of hypothetical propositions, one of the presuppositions of the truth-functional analysis of compound propositions is inapplicable; namely, the contention that the truth or falsity of any compound proposition is determined by the truth or falsity of its component propositions, and that the compound

[1] This is the standard, not the *only*, function of propositions of this form; cf. "If you want my opinion, he's a scoundrel", "If he is a puritan, he's certainly no prig", and Shakespeare's "If this be error and upon me proved, I never writ, nor no man ever loved", for which different accounts must be given.

proposition has a truth-value for *all* possible combinations of true and false in its component propositions. The truth-table for '$p \supset q$' is

p	q	$p \supset q$
T	T	T
T	F	F
F	T	T
F	T	T

But, since a hypothetical proposition asserts only what is the case if its antecedent is realised, its truth-table would be, at best,

p	q	if p,q
T	T	T
T	F	F

But even this will not do. Whereas, for '$p \cdot q$' to be true, it is enough that 'p' and 'q' should *each* be true, the truth of 'p' and 'q', taken separately, cannot guarantee the truth of 'if p, q', when the word 'if' is used in the standard way. In other words, propositions of the form 'if p, q' are not truth-functional.

The equivalence of '$p \supset q$', '$\sim p \lor q$' and '$\sim (p \cdot \sim q)$', in the system, calls for closer inspection. Now instead of saying "If it rains, the match will be cancelled", it is certainly possible for us to say, with no change of meaning, "Either it will not rain or the match will be cancelled" or "It will not rain without the match being cancelled". And those two variants seem to be accurately analysed as exemplifying the forms '$\sim p \lor q$' and '$\sim (p \cdot \sim q)$'. This conclusion is puzzling since, while, on the one hand, we have seen good reason to reject the equivalence of '$p \supset q$' with 'if p, q', it seems to be perfectly correct to substitute '$\sim p \lor q$' and '$\sim (p \cdot \sim q)$' for *either* '$p \supset q$' *or* 'if p, q'. How can this inconsistency, or apparent inconsistency, be resolved?

We remove it when we recognise that the proposition which we assert when we say "Either it will not rain or the match will be cancelled" does not, in spite of appearances, exemplify the form '$\sim p \lor q$'. '$\sim p \lor q$' is verified if either of the disjuncts is true; thus it is verified if '$\sim p$' is true. But "Either it will not rain or the match will be cancelled" does *not* express a proposition that is true if it does not rain, but one that is verified if it does rain and the match is cancelled, and falsified if it rains and the match is not cancelled. Thus, its truth-conditions are identical with those of 'if p, q' but not with those of '$p \supset q$' (or '$\sim p \vee q$' or '$\sim(p \cdot \sim q)$').[1] The truth-conditions of the proposition expressed as "It will not rain without the match being cancelled" are the same as those for the disjunctive proposition which we have considered.

As we have seen, '$\sim p \supset (p \supset q)$' and '$\sim p \supset (p \supset \sim q)$' are laws of the calculus. Provided that we read these formulae as their definitional equivalents, they present us with no paradox. So read, they can be reformulated as '$\sim \sim p \vee (\sim p \vee q)$' and '$\sim \sim p \vee (\sim p \vee q)$' (where the form '$P \supset Q$' is replaced by the form '$\sim P \vee Q$') or as '$\sim(\sim p \cdot \sim \sim(p \cdot \sim q))$' and '$\sim(\sim p \cdot \sim \sim(p \cdot \sim q))$' (where the form '$P \supset Q$' is replaced by the form '$\sim(P \cdot \sim Q)$'). We may readily agree that whatever proposition 'p' may be, either it is true or the disjunction of its contradictory and any other proposition whatsoever (e.g. 'q' or 'not-q') is true. But if we read the formulae as hypothetical, the resultant propositions seem to be unacceptable. There are no accepted arguments of the form 'If p is false, then, if it is (or if it were) true, any proposition whatsoever would be true'. Since, then, laws of the system which are paradoxical if read as hypotheticals cease to be paradoxical if read as conjunctive or disjunctive propositions, there is a strong temptation to 'save' the system by limiting the claim that is made on its behalf. Then we shall say something like this: "The calculus of propositions displays systematically the logical relations of those elementary propositions which involve negation, conjunction and disjunction; formulae employing the constant '$\supset$' are to be understood as abbreviations of formulae which employ the constants '$\cdot$', '$\vee$' and '$\sim$'." One might maintain further that, in itself, the formal relationship of antecedent-consequent generates no logical laws, or withdraw the claim that the calculus provides an analysis of the whole of propositional logic.

It has often been argued that, if we accept the doctrine of the

[1] The recognition that "Either it will not rain or the match will be cancelled" does *not* exemplify the form '$\sim p \vee q$' is a reminder of the dangers of too hastily identifying a proposition from the sentence which idiomatically is used to express it. We do not need to deny that sentences 'mean what they say'; but frequently something more than a cursory glance is needed if we are to grasp what they *do* say.

3+

calculus that a false proposition implies any statement whatsoever, we are bound to condemn as pointless or meaningless a very high proportion of the hypothetical assertions that we make in ordinary life, namely all those that are contrary to fact. Such a hypothetical proposition is 'If Hannibal had marched on Rome after Cannae, he would have taken it', which we make knowing that Hannibal did *not* march on Rome and did not take it. Nobody would wish to say that it follows from the fact that Hannibal did not march on Rome, that if he had marched on Rome he would have taken it, and equally that if he had marched on Rome he would not have taken it. The simplest way of meeting the implied criticism of the calculus is to say that counter-factual conditionals are to be analysed altogether differently from indicative conditionals and that, in Quine's words, "whatever the proper analysis of the counter-factual analysis may be, we may be sure in advance that it cannot be truth-functional". Then we should set aside any problem that they raise, perhaps on the ground that, again in Quine's words, it "belongs not to pure logic but to the theory of meaning or possibly the philosophy of science".[1] But it would be wrong to suppose that the impossibility of applying truth-functional analysis to such propositions marks a sharp distinction between them and indicative conditionals. There is a similar, though less acute, awkwardness about the application of the analysis to conditional propositions that are not contrary to fact. The stark intractability of counter-factual conditionals simply reveals the limitations of the analysis in a clearer light.

There is at least one other wide class of hypothetical propositions, the structure of which the calculus is or appears to be inadequate to present, namely such 'open' hypotheticals as 'If anyone smokes in a non-smoking compartment, he is liable to be fined', which are not constructed out of propositions which can be given a truth-value in isolation.[2] These we shall consider at a later stage but it is already clear that the straightforward truth-functional analysis demanded by

[1] W. V. Quine, *Methods of Logic*, 1952, pp. 14 and 15.

[2] Since "If it rains, the match will be cancelled" expresses *one* hypothetical proposition, a student *ought* to feel uneasy at the claim that the two clauses in the sentence express two propositions, which are true or false in isolation. In fact the claim becomes fully intelligible when propositions are distinguished from statements (see pp. 105–106). For the analysis of 'open' hypotheticals see p. 82.

the calculus cannot do full justice to the variety and complexity of hypothetical propositions in natural languages. Yet, in spite of this, the original claim, that it provides an analysis that is adequate for logical purposes, has not been shown to be false. It has not even been established that the respects in which hypothetical propositions are different from material implication propositions are of *logical* relevance.

Although we have noticed that it is impossible to mark the differences between counterfactual and other conditional propositions in the notation of the calculus, we have not shown in what way, if at all, those differences are relevant to the logical relations in which propositions of either type stand to other propositions. We have not shown, for example, that there are any distinct forms of implication which hold solely between counterfactual conditionals. Further, although we have seen that some laws of the calculus which involve the material implication sign are not acceptable as logical laws if the components involving '$\supset$' are read as hypotheticals, we have not shown that there are *not* laws in the calculus ('$\supset$-laws') to correspond with all laws expressed as hypotheticals ('if-laws'). Further, those '$\supset$-laws', such as '$\sim p \supset (p \supset q)$', which are not acceptable as 'if-laws', need not be rejected but may be read as laws of conjunction (or disjunction) and negation. In this guise no objection can be raised against them. Until logicians succeed in bringing to light laws of propositional logic which lie outside the system of the calculus (and which the notation of the calculus is inadequate to express), we may assume it to be satisfactory.

Before we leave the topic of the resemblances and differences between the constants of the calculus and the connectives of ordinary language, one point of disagreement among logicians may be noticed. In the propositional calculus, '$\sim p \supset p$' is a contingent formula. Being definitionally equivalent to '$\sim \sim p \lor p$' and '$\sim (\sim p \cdot \sim p)$', it yields a true compound proposition when a true proposition is substituted for 'p'. It is reasonable to ask, then, if the same can be said of 'if *not-p, p*'. To this question Łukasiewicz (with many other modern logicians) says yes, Aristotle no. Aristotle considered it was impossible that any proposition of the form 'if *not-p, p*' could be true. The argument for this view is clear. Hypothetical propositions state what is (or would be) the case if a given condition is satisfied. If, then, the condition expressed in the antecedent is '*not-p*', the realisation of that condition *precludes the possibility* of '*p*', for '*p*' and 'not-*p*' cannot, in accordance with the law of non-contradiction, both be true together. It could be a condition for a proposition being true that it was also false, only if it were logically possible for the same proposition to be both true and false. Łukasiewicz answered this argument (which he considered reveals ignorance of logic) by insisting that only '*p* and not-*p*', and *not* 'if not-*p*, *p*', is contrary to the law of non-contradiction.[1]

The explanation of the disagreement is not far to seek. For Łukasiewicz hypothetical propositions are *not* conditional. 'If *p*, *q*' does not, on his interpretation, state that on condition that '*p*' is realised, '*q*' is realised too. 'If *p*, *q*' has, for him, the meaning of '*p⊃q*' in the calculus; that is to say, it can be re-expressed as '$\sim p \vee q$' or '$\sim(p\cdot\sim q)$'. Aristotle is right. His intuitive rejection of the form 'if not-*p*, *p*' is not an error but emphasises in the clearest way the mistake of assuming without argument that '*p⊃q*' and 'if *p*, *q*' are synonymous formulae.

Logical impossibilities

The authors of the calculus, in treating the concept or idea of 'proposition' as primitive and undefined, appeal to our capacity to recognise those entities between which logical relations hold and which are true or false. And it is reasonable that they should do so. Proof presupposes *some* undemonstrated starting-points, and definition presupposes *some* undefined terms. But, in the calculus, not only '*p*', '*q*', '*r*' etc. and such compounds as '*p·q*', '*p⊃q*', '*p* ∨ *q*' are propositional forms but also '$p\cdot\sim p$' and '$\sim(p\cdot\sim p)$'. '$p\cdot\sim p$' is said to be logically false, while '$\sim(p\cdot\sim p)$' is logically true (or necessary). The admission of 'logically false propositions' to the calculus raises a difficulty which I shall briefly discuss.

What kind of a proposition is it that consists of the conjunction of a proposition and its negation, '$p\cdot\sim p$'? It is possible to make an assertion, then to retract it and substitute its negation. It is possible, too, to utter a sentence which apparently expresses the joint assertion and denial of the same thing; "It is and it isn't", for example, in answer to the question "Is the decoration of your room just as you

[1] J. Łukasiewicz, *op. cit.*, p. 50.

hoped it would be?''. But such sentences are not used to express propositions of the form '$p \cdot \sim p$' and are to be understood as roughly equivalent to "It is in some respects but it is not in other respects". Indeed we insist on such interpretations and refuse to admit the possibility that a man might jointly assert and, without retracting his assertion, at the same time and in the same respect deny the same thing. The 'proposition' that consists of the joint affirmation and negation of the same thing seems, then, not to be a proposition at all. A proposition is that which it is logically possible to conceive to be the case, so, if it is logically impossible to entertain a single proposition of the form '$p \cdot \sim p$', then the formula '$p \cdot \sim p$' cannot be a propositional form. Yet, as we have seen, in the calculus, '$p \cdot \sim p$' is a well-formed propositional formula, which has the truth-value False. Are we then to abandon our preconceptions of what we are entitled to call propositions? If we follow this course, we admit to the status of propositions expressions (or their meanings) which have no place in ordinary argument, and thereby a rift is created which threatens to separate the formulae of the calculus from the arguments of ordinary life. This consequence must be avoided if logic is to remain the analysis of what, independently of the study of logic, we recognise as valid arguments.

Yet to argue that there could be no proposition of the form '$p \cdot \sim p$' seems to have one disturbing consequence. '$\sim (p \cdot \sim p)$', which can be read as 'not both p and not-p', appears to be a straightforward formulation of the Law of Contradiction. At the same time it is, or seems to be, the negation of '$p \cdot \sim p$'. Must it not follow, then, that '$p \cdot \sim p$' is itself a proposition (or propositional form) and thus significant, if its negation is a significant propositional form? For if anything can be significantly denied, it must be possible for it to be significantly affirmed. So it would seem that, if '$p \cdot \sim p$' is to be rejected as expressing no proposition at all, '$\sim (p \cdot \sim p)$' must be likewise rejected.

One way out of the difficulty is to assert that there is a difference in kind between contingent formulae (e.g. '$p \cdot q$') and logically true and logically false formulae, but one that is not brought to light by the notation of the propositional calculus and other systems. One might argue that '$p \cdot \sim p$' is not to be understood as expressing a proposition, though a logically false one, but as a propositional schema that can never be significantly exemplified. So '$p \cdot \sim p$' would be, not the form of a class of propositions, but a form which *no* proposition could take. Then we could interpret ' $\sim (p \cdot \sim p)$', not as the negation of a significant propositional form, but as the denial of the possibility of propositions of the form '$p \cdot \sim p$'. Indeed, the law of non-contradiction is like a 'No Road' warning: it tells us, not that we *can* go along the road of '$p \cdot \sim p$', but that if we do so we shall always be wrong; it tells us rather that our way is blocked, that there is no such road to go down.

What seems to emerge is that since '$p \cdot \sim p$' is either a special sort of propositional form or not a propositional form at all, the function of the negative sign which precedes it in ' $\sim (p \cdot \sim p)$' is different from that of ' $\sim$ ' when it precedes a contingent formula, as in ' $\sim p$' or ' $\sim (p \cdot q)$'. That there is such a difference in function is reflected by the fact that we say, not "'p and not-p' is false", but that it is logically impossible for a proposition, 'p', and its negation, 'not-p', both to be true. However we interpret the formula, ' $\sim (p \cdot \sim p)$', we cannot, it seems, intelligibly describe it as the negation of a self-contradictory proposition. For a proposition to be significantly denied it must also be possible significantly to affirm it. But it is not a necessary condition of the significance of "It is logically impossible that 'p' and 'not-p' should both be true" that 'p and not-p' is significantly assertible. In fact the contrary is true.

The calculus and ordinary language

Historically, the systematisation of the logic of propositions forms part of an attempt at the end of the nineteenth century and at the beginning of the twentieth to show that mathematics can be derived from logical laws. "The primary aim of *Principia Mathematica* was to show that all pure mathematics follows from purely logical premisses and uses only concepts definable in logical terms."[1] Aristotle, on the other hand, seems to have been primarily concerned to bring to light the principles of argument involved in scientific proof, with his eye particularly on the biological sciences. But, in spite of differences in the aims of logicians, modern logic, of which the calculus of propositions is a part, is, as Eaton says, not dis-

[1] B. Russell, *My Philosophical Development*, 1959, p. 74.

continuous with Aristotelian logic.[1] Both are concerned to present systematically the principles in accordance with which propositions imply one another. The logic of propositions presents, systematically, logical laws which intuitively we can see to hold but which traditional logicians either failed to recognise altogether or misrepresented as belonging to the logic of terms. Both systems of logic must satisfy the same criteria if they are to stand. As was said before, the same appeal is made to our capacity to distinguish valid from invalid argument. If 'All S is P' does not entail 'Some S is P', the traditional doctrine that A-propositions entail I-propositions must be rejected. If 'if not-p, p' is a logical absurdity, the claim that the relation between antecedent and consequent is adequately represented by '⊃' must be disallowed.

Mr Strawson contrasts the exact and systematic logic of, for example, the propositional calculus with the 'logic of expressions of everyday speech'.[2] He compares the formal logician constructing a logical system to a map-maker who, though ostensibly mapping a piece of country, insists on using in his drawings only geometrical figures for which rules of construction can be given and whose maps in consequence will never quite fit. Such a comparison is, I think, misleading. Only if the axioms of the calculus are necessary truths, and only if its constants express propositional negation and those relations between propositions which, without any specialised knowledge of the technical vocabulary of logic, we can see to be logically relevant, is the calculus a system of logic at all. If those conditions are not satisfied, the axioms are rules, as distinct from laws, and hold good only because the inventor of the system has laid it down that they shall hold. Such rules would be no more logical rules than are the rules for games like chess or bridge.

Yet, it is worth repeating, even if the axioms of the calculus were of the same status as rules of games, proofs within the system could only be carried out in accordance with principles that were not merely rules but laws that, without reference to the system, we recognise as valid. One may prescribe what are to be the premisses of an argument but not what is to constitute a valid argument from those premisses. So the principles of inference must be common both

1 R. M. Eaton, *op. cit.*, p. 2.
2 P. F. Strawson, *Introduction to Logical Theory*, 1952, pp. 57 and 58.

to the arguments of everyday life and to symbolic systems if any operations within those systems are to be called proofs or demonstrations. In fact, as I have said, the calculus of propositions claims to be a genuine system of logic. Both the principles of inference involved and the axioms (and, in consequence, the theorems) are to be thought of as necessary laws of implication which hold for all thought however expressed, whether in a special vocabulary or in natural languages. That, over and above the logic of the calculus, there is a further 'logic of expressions of everyday speech' is a view which will be indirectly opposed in Chapter 6.

4

EXISTENCE, PREDICATION AND IDENTITY

We have already seen that there are defects in the traditional analysis of propositions. In the main, these stem from the belief that all propositions are of subject-predicate form. Once we have recognised that this belief is mistaken, we can understand the strength and importance of more recent analyses of the logic of terms. In this chapter I shall attempt to show that both propositions of existence and propositions of identity are to be distinguished from true subject-predicate propositions, and I shall survey briefly the range of propositions of each of these three kinds.

It is not surprising that many philosophers in the past have assumed, not always critically, that all propositions can be analysed into subjects and predicates. Respect for the authority of Aristotle had the effect of ensuring that, while formal logic remained a cardinal subject in European education, any radical re-examination of its doctrines was stifled. It was assumed even by so critical and original a philosopher as Kant that the traditional analysis of propositions was complete and called for no modification or improvement. Further, the dead weight of authority was reinforced by the initial plausibility of the Aristotelian analysis. The sentences in which we express propositions usually have grammatical subjects, and it is easy, and often correct, to assume that the function of the grammatical subject is to refer to whatever the proposition expressed is about. At the same time, we naturally tend to assume that every proposition is about *something*. In fact, if we understand the phrase 'about something' in a very wide sense, we can always find *an* answer to the question, "What is such-and-such a proposition about?" Thus, for example, one may say that the proposition,

'It is raining', is about the weather, that 'God exists' is about God, that 'If Hannibal had marched on Rome after Cannae, he would have taken it' is about Hannibal or, in a general way, about the military situation in Italy at a certain time in Roman history. Yet acceptance of the traditional doctrine makes it impossible to formulate a system of the formal logic of terms that is both adequate and consistent.

If, in answer to the enquiry, "May I speak to your wife?", I say "She is visiting a friend", I do not assert that I *have* a wife. Nor would it be apposite for me to say that I had. For the form of the enquirer's question makes it clear that he knows that I am married. So the function of the word 'She' in my answer is to refer to a particular—and of course *existing*—person. Our conversation did not start with knowledge on one side and blank ignorance on the other. Both of us start from the knowledge that I am married, that there is someone who is married to me. From consideration of situations such as this, we may come to understand the place of subject-predicate propositions in the pattern of our assertions. Their use presupposes some prior knowledge of what exists and they therefore occur, as it were, not at the beginning but in the middle of our discourse. When our statements are of subject-predicate form the things or persons about which we speak are already 'given'. That there are such things or persons it is not the function of those propositions to express. Yet that there are such things or persons is a precondition for what appear to be subject-predicate propositions being subject-predicate propositions at all, which can be true or false.

But not all the statements we make are about things the existence of which is already given and unquestioned. Sometimes we need to introduce, as it were, to our audience those persons or things about which we shall afterwards make further assertions. Then, like the writers of fairy-tales, we start, not in the middle, but at the beginning —"Once upon a time there was a King. Now the King had three beautiful daughters." The first of these sentences expresses in a very easily recognisable form just such an 'introductory' proposition; it is not predicative but existential. In it we are not told anything *about* a King, only that there *is* a King for predicative statements, like the one that follows it, to be about. It is clear that sometimes we need to make statements of this kind.

Existential propositions are expressed most unambiguously in sentences which begin with such phrases as "There is . . .", "Once upon a time there were . . ." But, perhaps unfortunately for the history of logical analysis, there is no one distinguishable way of expressing them, and no philosopher has yet succeeded in winning universal acceptance for the principles that he has advocated for distinguishing existential propositions from those of other kinds. It is with the classification which is presupposed by the system of the logic of terms called the 'calculus of predicates' that we shall be principally concerned in this chapter. Yet there is some ground of common agreement and this we shall cover first.

Existence is not a predicate. The sentence, "God exists", is of grammatically subject-predicate form; 'God' is the subject and 'exists' the predicate. But the proposition which that sentence is most naturally used to express is not predicative. As we have seen, it is a precondition of a proposition being predicative that there is something which is its subject. If "God exists" expressed such a proposition, then the function of the word 'God' would be to refer to an existing being—namely God, whose existence would thus be presupposed. But, in that case, "God exists" would express an empty truism to the effect that God, to whom reference is made and who therefore exists, exists. But "God exists" does not express a self-guaranteeing truth of logic but a significantly contradictable proposition. How, then, are we to analyse it?

Here it will help us to consider our ordinary language. Instead of saying "God exists", we could say instead "There is a God". Further, if we wished to contradict the original proposition, we should say "There is no God", not "No, he does not exist". But "There is a God" and "There is no God" appear unambiguously to express existential propositions. Since, then, the contradictory of the original proposition is existential and it itself can be expressed in a sentence used to express an existential proposition, it too is an existential proposition though expressed in a sentence of subject-predicate form. Misleadingly, sentences expressing both predicative and existential propositions can be of the same grammatical form. In "God exists" the word 'God' is not used as a proper name to refer to an (existing) individual being but rather as an abbreviated description. The sentence is used to express a proposition to the effect that a divine being exists or, in other words, that there is a divine being. (The precise meaning of the words 'God' and 'divine' in a given context will depend, of course, on the theological views of the speaker.) Parallel alternative versions cannot be given of sentences that express genuinely subject-predicate propositions. 'God is just' presupposes that there is a God, but is not the same proposition as 'There is a just God', while the contradictory of 'God is just' is 'God (or 'He') is not just'. In the sentence, "God is just", by contrast with "God exists", 'God' is used as a proper name to refer uniquely to one individual. Thus it is that the word 'exist' is commonly used in predicative sentences which express propositions that are not predicative; and it may be useful to notice some of the conditions in which it can be so used. We may say "Tigers exist" or "Tame tigers exist" but to say "The tiger over there exists" and "That tame tiger exists" is to overstep the line that separates sense from nonsense. Why such sentences are nonsensical should be clear from the argument; we use the phrase 'That tame tiger' to *individuate* a particular animal, to fix the subject of which predicates may be asserted (e.g. "That tame tiger was born in captivity").

It is impossible to list exhaustively all the different ways in which existential and predicative propositions are expressed in English and other natural languages in which the same verb is used to express both predication and existence, as in "There is a God" and "God is just". We are less likely to make a mistaken analysis if, when confronted with a logically ambiguous sentence, we ask ourselves "What thing (if anything) is here *referred to* and what is asserted about it?" But there is no magic in the question to dissolve all our difficulties. Above all, to the question "What is the hallmark of a referring expression?" we soon find ourselves needing a clearer answer than common-sense and the procedure of ₊ooking for synonymous sentences and asking a few straightforward uestions can provide. On the answer that we give to this question or, rather, on the conclusions that we reach about what are and what are not referring expressions, will depend our acceptance or rejection of the analyses of propositions that logicians, from Aristotle onwards, have put forward.

For traditional logic, phrases like 'All men' and 'Some men', as well as proper names like 'Socrates' and 'London', are referring expressions, and the propositions which are expressed in sentences having such words and phrases as their subjects are subject-predicate propositions. Similarly, 'No men are immortal' and 'Nobody is immortal' are thought to be of the same form even when no definite decision is reached as to whether 'No men' and 'Nobody' are strictly referring expressions. The function of words like 'someone', 'anyone', 'nothing' is not always fully considered, and the difficulties which they raise do not seem to have shaken the confidence of traditionalists in their analysis of propositions. But in the present century two theories have provided the impetus for the re-examination of the analysis of propositions, and, at the same time, have largely determined the lines which that re-examination has followed. The first of these is the theory of 'propositional functions', which originates in the investigations of the mathematical philosopher Frege and the mathematician Peano into the possibility of deriving mathematics from logical axioms. We are here only concerned with the theory for the light that it throws on the analysis of general propositions.

A propositional function is a schema such as 'x is mortal' which can be converted into a proposition by the substitution of a determinate *value* (e.g. 'Socrates') for 'x'. It was claimed by Russell (who borrowed the theory from Peano and saw its importance for logic) that, even if such propositions as 'Socrates is mortal' are subject-predicate propositions about named subjects, general propositions (i.e. those the expression of which involves such words as 'some' and 'all' in their grammatical subjects) state connections between propositional functions. Thus, on this view, 'All men are mortal' is a proposition to the effect that whatever x may be, if x is a man, x is mortal.

The second of the two theories, which we owe entirely to Russell, is his Theory of Descriptions and consists of his views on the function, in sentences expressing propositions, of descriptive phrases introduced by 'the' and 'a', the definite and indefinite articles. The influence of these theories on twentieth-century logical analysis can hardly be overestimated. Although I shall not attempt here to present them as Russell has presented them, nor even to note the points at which the argument follows a different line and arrives at a different conclusion from his, they largely determine the form that the following discussion will take.

Subject-predicate propositions

Let us first consider such singular propositions with named subjects as 'Socrates is mortal'. Few would be inclined to deny that this is of subject-predicate form. It is a precondition of a proposition being of subject-predicate form that the subject-word or -phrase denotes a person or thing which exists, has existed, or, perhaps, will exist. This condition, we may argue, is here satisfied, for the word 'Socrates' is the name of a real individual.

What then of such other proper names as 'Pickwick', 'Hamlet' or 'Cerberus'? Does the fact that Pickwick is a character in fiction, that Hamlet (we may suppose, for the sake of argument) was not a historical person but a creature of Shakespeare's imagination, disqualify them from being subjects of propositions? Russell gives a clear answer to this question. To argue that they are not disqualified reveals, he considers, "a failure of that feeling for reality which ought to be preserved even in the most abstract studies." "Logic", he maintains, "should no more admit a unicorn than zoology can." "To maintain that Hamlet, for example, exists in his own world, namely, in the world of Shakespeare's imagination . . . is to say something deliberately confusing, or else confused to a degree that is hardly credible. There is only one world, the real world."[1]

The implication of Russell's view is that at best only those things could be logical subjects which are physical components of the world. Characters in novels, heraldic beasts, gods and heroes in classical mythology are thereby excluded, and one wonders if the 'robust sense of reality' which Russell demands is not too robust. On the view argued, it would seem to follow that 'John signed Magna Carta' is a subject-predicate proposition, while 'Hamlet killed Polonius' is not, and that for the latter to be a significant proposition and thereby something that can be true or false, it must be one of a different kind. This, presumably, would be something like 'There was once someone called Hamlet and he killed Polonius',

[1] B. Russell, *Introduction to Mathematical Philosophy*, 1919, ch. 16.

which, since there was no such person as Hamlet, is a straight-forwardly false existential statement.

We can partly account for Russell's views on fiction and the statements of myth and legend. They seem to reflect, in part, his reaction against the view of Meinong, a German philosopher whose work he had respected, that since "we can speak about 'the golden mountain', 'the round square' and so on" and since "we can make true propositions of which these are the subjects", they must possess "some kind of logical being, since otherwise the propositions in which they occur would be meaningless". Yet it is clear that phrases like 'the round square' are importantly different in kind from names like 'Hamlet' or such descriptive phrases as 'the man in the iron mask'. We may say that the sentence, "I drew a round square yesterday", *taken as a whole*, is meaningless. 'Round square' is a contradiction in terms and, unless special meanings are given to either of the words that make it up, it can have no possible reference. We have, then, no incentive to assert propositions of which 'the round square' is the logical subject. But the laws of logic do not rule out the possibility of—for example—unicorns, and so long as we recognise that unicorns are legendary and heraldic monsters, there is no harm in saying that there are such things in the 'universe of heraldry' or the 'universe of legend' as the case may be. When we make statements about Mr Pickwick we are, in a wide sense, making statements about the *Pickwick Papers*, and they are statements which can be straightforwardly verified or falsified by reference to the novel. To accept the claim that true statements can be made, the subjects of which are the characters of fiction or legend, is not to put one's foot on the slippery slope that leads to the invention of imaginary worlds in which there are round squares. When there is any danger that confusion may arise we can, and do, locate the reference of our discourse by such phrases as 'in Dickens's novel', 'in Greek mythology', 'in medieval romances'.

There is perhaps a more important reason for Russell's rejection of Hamlet, Mr Pickwick and, in general, fictional or legendary characters as possible logical subjects. He is concerned with the logical structure of scientific discourse, and there is no place in the 'real world' for the fictional. Perhaps for this reason he is reluctant to conceal the difference in ontological status between propositions about real people and things and those about fictional characters, by admitting what we should naturally call fictional subject-predicate propositions to be of the same logical form as those the subjects of which belong to the real world. But, as we have seen, when propositions about fiction are in danger of being misunderstood as propositions about science and history, we can prevent confusion by such qualifications as I have mentioned. Thus, so far as logic is concerned, I should maintain that 'Socrates is mortal' and 'Hamlet was indecisive' are of the same, subject-predicate, form.

Propositional functions

Let us next consider general propositions, namely those that traditional logic classified as of the A, E, I and O forms. It is contended by Russell, as we have seen, that all such propositions assert connections between propositional functions. Thus the propositions 'All men are mortal', 'No men are mortal', 'Some men are mortal' and 'Some men are not mortal' are analysed thus: 'Whatever x may be, if x is a man, x is mortal', 'Whatever x may be, if x is a man, x is not mortal', 'There is an x such that x is a man and x is mortal', 'There is an x such that x is a man and x is not mortal'.[1]

The proposition, 'All men are mortal', is one of unrestricted generality; it asserts that being mortal is involved in being a man. It is not about particular individual men; it is about whoever or whatever satisfies the condition of 'being a man' or, we may say, the *concept* of 'man'. Thus, instead of using the standard form of words, we can say "Whatever is a man is mortal" or "If anything is a man it is mortal". When we make such an assertion, we assert nothing of Tom, Dick or Harry, although to understand the sense of what is said is to recognise that if Tom, Dick and Harry satisfy the defining conditions of being men, then they exemplify the universal proposition, provided that it is true. In fact, we neither assert nor deny that the proposition is instantiated. At the same time, we normally use the indicative mood to express universal propositions only when there

[1] One minor merit of the new analysis will be readily admitted. A single counter-example is enough to falsify a universal proposition; that one man is not mortal contradicts the proposition that all men are mortal. Thus the elimination of the implication of plurality conveyed by the traditional formulae, 'Some S is P', 'Some S is not P', is, so far as it goes, a point in favour of the form 'There is an x such that, etc.'

exist in fact things that satisfy the description which the grammatical subject provides. Thus, if I said "Dodos cannot fly", I should be understood to think that there are still dodos in existence. It is clear, however, that universal propositions can be expressed in forms of words that do not entitle us to draw such a conclusion. If we are in doubt whether there are, or are confident that there are not, perfect liquids, we might say, instead of "A perfect liquid is frictionless" (a more natural form of expression than "All perfect liquids are frictionless"), "A perfect liquid would be frictionless" or "If there are any perfect liquids, they are (or must be) frictionless". Moreover, to say "Offenders against the bye-laws are liable to prosecution" is not to suggest that offences against the bye-laws have (or have not) been committed.

Yet it may be said that, since universal propositions expressed in the indicative mood normally presuppose the existence of instances, a formulation that does not reflect this presupposition provides a distorted and inaccurate analysis. To meet this objection we must examine the notion of 'presuppositions' more closely; in particular it will be useful to compare the 'presuppositions' of unquestionable subject-predicate propositions with those of universal propositions.

For the sentence, "John Smith is president of the Cricket Club", to express a subject-predicate proposition it is necessary, as we have already seen, that there is such a person as John Smith. This precondition is not to be explained as arising from any sort of *convention*. In other words, it is not a *linguistic* rule, or a matter of current idiom, that, if some person or thing is referred to, there must *be* such a person or thing to be referred to. This in no way contradicts what was said earlier about subject-predicate propositions with fictional subjects; there *is* such a person as Pickwick—in the *Pickwick Papers*. It is logically necessary that if there were no such person as John Smith no propositions could be formulated of which John Smith was the logical subject.[1] But we cannot give a similar account of the 'existential presupposition' of universal propositions. At most we can say that it is misleading to express such propositions in the indicative except when the 'subject-class' is instantiated. Moreover, even if it were idiomatically impermissible to use the indicative

[1] The logical subject of a proposition about John Smith is John Smith, not the *name* 'John Smith'.

mood in English for expressing uninstantiated universal propositions, it could not be seriously maintained that such a rule of language
must hold for the expression of universal propositions in *any*
language or even that some universal propositions must be expressed
in the indicative mood. Just as there is no logical absurdity in the
notion of propounding what would be the properties of perfect
liquids, if any such existed, so there is no logical absurdity in
supposing that no such linguistic convention held in English or any
other language. To have provided an analysis of universal propositions which makes no allowance for the presumption that they are in
fact instantiated is a merit and not a defect of the Russellian analysis
which we are considering. The universal proposition, 'All men are
mortal', does not entail that some men are mortal, and the logician
is in error if he misdescribes as a relation of logical necessity what is
no more than a presumption authorised by the linguistic conventions
of a particular language.

The grammatical subjects of universal propositions, however
expressed, are not referring expressions. The Russellian formula
'For all x, if x is f, x is g' makes explicit the function of such words
as 'whoever', 'anyone who', 'whatever', etc. as they are used in
common speech. When we say 'Whatever is human is mortal', we
assert that any instance of 'man' (i.e. anything of which 'being a
man' can be predicated) is also an instance of mortality, without
committing ourselves to a decision on whether or not 'being a man'
is in fact predicable of anything. Earlier logicians came close to
Russell's account when they argued that universal propositions
assert a relation between universal concepts or recognised them as
disguised open hypothetical propositions. By 'open' hypotheticals I
mean such propositions as 'If anyone has influenza, he should have
medical attention' (which we may express as "All influenza patients
should have medical attention"); they are contrasted with 'closed'
hypotheticals such as 'If George has influenza, he should have
medical attention'. In the language of propositional functions,
'George' is a *value* for x in the expression, 'If x is an influenza
patient, x should have medical attention'.

The Russellian analysis of the traditional I and O propositions
in terms of propositional functions is equally acceptable. To assert
the contradictory of 'All men are mortal' is to assert that there is at

least one x, such that x is a man and x is not mortal or, more briefly, that there is at least one man who is not mortal. On this view, subject-phrases such as 'some men', 'somebody', 'at least one man', 'something' are no more referring expressions than 'all men'.

Consideration of common language confirms this analysis. If a conspirator said "Somebody has given us away" and meant the sentence in its usual sense, he would not thereby refer to any particular individual. What he asserts is simply that there *is* some individual who has betrayed the plot. Thus it would not be appropriate to contradict him with the words, "No, he has not given us away". Such a rejoinder has the same absurdity for the same reasons as "No, he does not", uttered as a negative response to "God exists". The usual expression of the contradictory of the proposition is "Nobody has given us away". And 'nobody' and 'nothing' are no more individuating or referring expressions than 'somebody' and 'something'. In the *Odyssey*, Ulysses told the Cyclops Polyphemus that his name was Noman. Later he blinded Polyphemus and made his escape, whereupon Polyphemus called to the other Cyclopes for help, and the answer which he gave when they asked who had blinded him was that Noman had done it—an answer that they not unreasonably interpreted as equivalent to "There is no man who has done it". So to say "Nobody has given us away" is to say that there is not anyone who has given us away or, in the language of the analysis which we are considering, 'There is not an x such that x is a man and x has given us away'. Of course there might be an occasion when, to "Somebody has given us away", either the question, "To whom are you referring?", or the response, "No, he has not", might be appropriate rejoinders; as, for example, when the questioner recognises that the speaker is saying less than he is in a position to say. But even if a man were to say "Somebody has given us away" knowing who the traitor was, 'somebody' would still not be a referring expression.

Definite and indefinite descriptions

Russell claimed that propositions expressed in sentences the grammatical subjects of which are definite or indefinite descriptive phrases are general propositions: in other words, that they are of the same forms as those the subjects of which are 'All'-phrases or 'Some'-phrases.

So far as indefinite descriptions are concerned the claim is justified. If 'Someone has given us away' is correctly analysed as existential, so too is 'A traitor has given us away'. "A schoolmaster should be patient" is a variant of "All schoolmasters should be patient" and hence of "Whatever x may be, if x is a schoolmaster, x should be patient". Similarly, "A schoolmaster punished the boy" is a variant of "There is an x such that x is a schoolmaster and x punished the boy". For a descriptive phrase that begins with the indefinite article we can always substitute a phrase which begins with the word 'some' or 'any' or 'all'.

But the Russellian analysis of propositions expressed in sentences the grammatical subjects of which are definite descriptions (i.e. descriptive phrases introduced by the word 'the') has been much criticised. Russell's view is that "the only thing that distinguishes 'the so-and-so' from 'a so-and-so' is the implication of uniqueness", and that every proposition of which the apparent subject is 'the so-and-so' is a general proposition. Some objections to this view are obvious. It is implausible to suggest that the only difference between "A man met me at the station" and "The man whom we were talking about met me at the station" lies in the (alleged) fact that the proposition expressed in the first sentence does not exclude the possibility that more than one man met me, whereas that expressed by the second does. It is also initially implausible to argue that both sentences express existential propositions. Whereas the first is of the form, 'There is an x such that x is a man and x met me at the station', the latter appears to be irreducibly predicative. 'The man whom we were talking about' seems to have the same function in the context as a proper name would have.

Definite descriptions, occurring as the subjects of sentences, have at least two distinct functions, which may be illustrated by two sets of examples:

1. 'The Prime Minister presides at Cabinet meetings'
   'The Sovereign of Great Britain is the head of the Commonwealth'
   'The man who wrote this unsigned letter had a bad pen'

2. 'The Prime Minister has invited me to lunch'
   'The Queen made a tour of the Commonwealth'
   'The author of *Waverley* limped'

It is not difficult to see that the grammatical subjects of the sentences quoted in List 1 are not used—as proper names, for example, are used—to refer uniquely. For 'The Prime Minister' and 'The Sovereign' we can substitute, without change of meaning, 'Whoever is Prime Minister' and 'Whoever is Sovereign' or, more awkwardly, 'All Prime Ministers' and 'All British Sovereigns'. It is to be noticed, too, that the definite article here carries the implication of uniqueness, and we may contrast the implications of 'The Prime Minister presides at Cabinet meetings' with those of 'A senior member of the Government presides at Cabinet meetings'. With the sentences in List 2 the case is different. The subject-phrases serve to identify individuals, and what is predicated in each case is predicated of the individuals so identified. If proper names were substituted for the subject-phrases, the resulting propositions would be of the same form.

The correct analysis of propositions expressed in sentences the subjects of which are definite descriptions is much in dispute, and many logicians would be dissatisfied with the two-fold distinction which I have drawn. Indeed there is no general agreement about what the facts are that need to be explained. Russell's theory was designed to explain, among other things, how it comes about that we can significantly assert "The author of *Waverley* exists" but not "Scott exists". But if, as seems to be the case, Russell is mistaken, if, that is to say, we do not have a use for sentences such as "The author of *Waverley* exists", no theory is called for to explain how they come to be significant.

Except on those occasions when our use of definite descriptions is of the kind illustrated by the sentences in List 1, the usual function of 'the' is to single out individuals. There is an exact analogy between this use of definite descriptions and the standard use of proper names. Thus we do not need to explain how it is that we can say "The author of *Waverley* exists". We cannot significantly say it any more than we can significantly say "Scott exists" and for the same reason. We do not give proper names to every pebble in the sea-shore, but this does not prevent us from making predicative assertions about any individual pebble. When we do so we individuate by describing and pointing instead of by naming.

In general, then, the propositions which we are considering are to be analysed in one of two ways, either as subject-predicate propositions, or as propositions of the form, 'For all x, if x is f, x is g' (where 'f' and 'g' are predicate-variables). But it is not surprising that some propositions accommodate themselves awkwardly to these two frameworks. "The person who wrote this letter had a bad pen" can be expressed as "Whoever wrote this letter had a bad pen"; but the formulation, "For all x, if x wrote this letter, x had a bad pen", is less acceptable, since propositions of this form can be true even if uninstantiated. 'The man who wrote this letter had a bad pen' and 'Nobody wrote this letter' are logically inconsistent propositions, while 'For all x, if x wrote this letter, x had a bad pen' and 'Nobody wrote this letter' are not inconsistent. The phrases "The man who wrote this letter", "The author of *Waverley*" (*or* "The man who wrote *Waverley*") could only be used to express the subjects of subject-predicate propositions if someone did write the letter in question and if someone did write *Waverley*. These are not merely conventional presuppositions. Their truth is a genuine precondition of the two quoted sentences expressing propositions at all; and, to represent the logical status of such propositions, neither the traditional analysis nor the analysis in terms of propositional functions, 'For all x, if x is f, x is g', is adequate by itself. Either a new analysis is demanded or the presupposition must be made explicit by the addition of some such phrase as 'and there is an x such that x is f'.

Some logicians, while agreeing that propositions of unrestricted generality (e.g. 'All men are mortal') are to be analysed in terms of propositional functions, have doubted if the same analysis holds for those that, in a wide sense of 'about', are about all the members of a limited class. It is, as Strawson has pointed out, paradoxical that the propositions 'Jack Straw is happy' and 'All the Straws are happy' should be said to exemplify different logical forms, namely, 'a is g' and 'For all x, if x is f, x is g' (where 'f' stands for 'being a member of the Straw family'). Yet although the Straw family consists of members who can be enumerated, the second proposition is not about named individuals but about *whoever* are members of the family, about, that is to say, all those x's for which 'x is a member of the Straw family' is true. So perhaps we should accept the paradox and agree to the assimilation of all such propositions to the form, 'For all x, if x is f, x is g', with or without the addition, 'and there is an x such that x is f'. And perhaps it is too much to expect that all the propositions which men have occasion to assert in natural languages should fall, without some awkwardness, into a narrow range of accepted logical forms. Anxiety on the part of the logical analyst to allow for subtle differences between expressions in a given language can have the effect of robbing his system of universality.

So far we have only considered the application of the analysis of propositions in terms of propositional functions to cases where x is a so-called 'individual variable'. In the language of the predicative calculus,[1] we 'quantify over' variables when we assert that, for all x or for some x, 'x is f' is true. But the analysis can be illuminatingly extended to cover all kinds of propositions concerned with totalities and instances, propositions, that is to say, in the expression of which the words 'all' and 'some' and such words as 'whenever' and 'whatever' are used.

Thus, 'This wine has all the virtues of good claret' can be analysed as 'For all f, if f is a virtue of a good claret, f is possessed by this wine'; and, here we quantify over a predicate-variable. Again, 'Whenever John argues he loses his temper' is of the form, 'For all t, if t is a time when John argues, t is a time when John loses his temper'; and 'Harry is cheerful in all situations' is of the form, 'For all s, if s is a situation in which Harry finds himself, s is a situation in which Harry is cheerful'. The cumbrousness and verbal absurdity of these formulations should not blind us to the fact that they reveal the true function of the suffix '-ever' (as in 'whatever', 'whenever', 'whoever') and of such words as 'all' or 'some'. These reformulations will not seem absurd when we recognise that they are intended not to replace but to explain the more succinct forms of expression that have developed in natural languages.

Identity-propositions

It remains for us to examine the use of names, definite

[1] See p. 94.

descriptions and indefinite descriptions as the grammatical predicates of sentences. Let us first consider the following examples:

> "Scott wrote books"
> "Scott was an author"
> "Scott was the author of *Waverley*"

The first sentence expresses a proposition of subject-predicate form,[1] but how are we to classify the second and third? From one point of view the second sentence groups itself with the first in that they are almost, if not quite, synonymous. At the same time the second sentence may seem to differ in kind from the third only in respect of the fact that the phrase 'the author of *Waverley*' carries, while 'an author' does not, the 'implication of uniqueness'. To assert that Scott was the author of *Waverley* implies that he alone wrote it: to assert that he was an author does not exclude the possibility that other people too are authors. Yet in this respect the second sentence seems to be analogous to the first. To ascribe a predicate to one thing is not to exclude the possibility that the same predicate can be ascribed to other things. So let us compare the first sentence and the second more closely.

To say that Scott wrote books is to characterise him or, in a loose sense of the word, to *describe* him: to say that he was an author is to say that he is an individual of a certain kind, or to ascribe him to a class of individuals. This distinction between predicative propositions and class-membership propositions is a fine one that, from a logical point of view, is sometimes unimportant. "If all men are mortal and Socrates is a man, then he is mortal" and "If all human beings are mortal and Socrates is human, then he is mortal" seem to be simply linguistic variants expressing the same proposition. But if one were asked what ground one had for asserting that a particular pillar-box was a red object (a class-membership proposition), one might be driven to say "Because it is red, of course", but one could not reasonably proffer as a ground for asserting that it was red, "Because it is a red object". Membership of a class is determined by predication, so predication seems in some sense to be 'logically prior' to class-membership.

---

[1] This is not to deny that it also exemplifies a relational form, in which 'Scott' and 'books' are the related terms.

A correct analysis of the proposition expressed in the sentence, "Scott was the author of *Waverley*", can only be made if we understand, at least in part, the difference in function between proper names and descriptions. The primary function of a proper name is to refer to an individual person or thing. The proper name 'Scott' occurs in its primary function in the sentence, "Scott wrote books", but not in the sentence, "'Scott' is a Scottish name". In order completely to understand a sentence in which a proper name occurs in its primary function, it is necessary to know to what the name applies, i.e. what it names, or stands for. Indeed, if there is nothing which a combination of letters, purporting to be a name occurring in its primary function, names, it is without significance but simply a noise or a mark on paper. On the other hand, it is not a precondition of our understanding a definite description that we should know to what or whom the description applies, nor is the description meaningless if there *is* nothing to which it applies. Though no man has visited the moon, the definite description, 'the first man to visit the moon', is a significant phrase. If this were not so, if the same general conditions for the significance of proper names held for definite descriptions also, then the sentence, "Scott was the author of *Waverley*", could only be recognised as *significant* by me if 'the author of *Waverley*' referred to a named individual and I knew what individual it named.

We can put this more simply. If the conditions for the significance of proper names and of descriptions were the same, then, if someone said to me "Scott is the author of *Waverley*", I could not understand *what he meant* unless I knew already that the phrase 'the author of *Waverley*' named or did not name the same man as is named 'Scott'. We may go further: if the phrase 'the author of *Waverley*' were significant because, and only in so far as, it named the same man that the name 'Scott' names, then to say "Scott was the author of *Waverley*" would be to assert the same proposition, though expressed in different words, as is expressed by "Scott was Scott". But, of course, to say that Scott was the author of *Waverley* is not to state a tautology but a contingently true proposition.

We have already noticed some of the ways in which descriptive phrases are used. In such a sentence as "The pebble in the bucket is smooth", the definite description is a substitute for a proper name;

but it individuates not by naming, but by describing. In "The Prime Minister presides at Cabinet meetings" the definite description is not used to refer to an unnamed or nameless individual but can be replaced by the phrase "Whoever is the Prime Minister" or, in more technical language, "For all *x*, if *x* is the Prime Minister, *x* etc.". But what is the function of definite descriptions occurring in the grammatical predicates of sentences, as in "Harold Macmillan is the Prime Minister" or "Scott is the author of *Waverley*"? This is a use to which we have already been introduced in the reformulation of "The Prime Minister presides at Cabinet Meetings"; that is to say, in "Whoever *is the Prime Minister* presides at Cabinet Meetings".

To understand this use we must consider again points raised in what was said about "Scott was an author". First, we should notice that there are two different functions of the verb 'to be' in indicative sentences. One function is illustrated in "Scott is lame", the other in "Scott is the author of *Waverley*". For Scott to be lame is for a *general* quality, attribute or characteristic to be predicable of him. For Scott to be the author of *Waverley* is for him to be *one particular individual*. This second use of the verb 'to be' is exemplified by sentences in which the predicate consists of some part of the verb 'to be' together with descriptions, definite or indefinite, or proper names. The propositions which they express may be called propositions of identity.

Why the word 'identity' in this connection is potentially misleading is clear if we consider again the sentence, "Scott is an author". While this sentence expresses the fact that Scott is an individual, a member of a class of individuals, it does not identify him as a *particular* individual (e.g. as the author who lived at Abbotsford). It might then be less misleading to distinguish, on the one hand, predicative propositions and, on the other, propositions which assert that something is an individual, whether a particular individual or a member of a class of individuals. Then we could include in a subdivision those that can be described unambiguously as propositions of identity, and these will consist of those expressed in sentences the predicates of which are either names or definite descriptions.

By the sentence, "Scott was the author of *Waverley*", we assert that an individual referred to by the proper name 'Scott' is the one individual of whom it was true that he wrote *Waverley*. Of course we do not assert that the words 'Scott' and 'the author of Waverley' have the same meaning but that the individual whom we name can be identified as the individual who wrote *Waverley*. 'Scott', then, is the name by which I refer to the individual about whom I am asserting— I am, of course, not asserting anything about the *name* 'Scott'. The phrase, 'the author of *Waverley*', is what I shall call a singularly descriptive expression and to assert that Scott is the author of *Waverley* is to assert that he 'satisfies' this singularly descriptive expression. Of course we can use the expressions 'Scott' and 'the author of *Waverley*' to refer to the same individual. Indeed, if we could not do so the sentence, "Scott was the author of *Waverley*", would not express a true proposition. But in this sentence it is not the function of 'the author of *Waverley*' to refer.[1]

When we say that Scott was lame we may be said to ascribe 'being lame' to Scott. So when we say that Scott was the author of *Waverley* we may be said to ascribe 'being the individual who wrote *Waverley*' to Scott. But it is no more the case that the second, any more than the first, of these ascriptions constitutes a reference to, or naming of, any individual. It would seem to be impossible for a sentence of the form, "(Proper name) is (definite description)" or "(Definite description) is (definite description)", to be used to express a proposition at all if the function of both the linked expressions were to refer. This contention, however, should not be misunderstood. When we ascribe 'being the individual who wrote *Waverley*' to Scott we do not predicate. I predicate something of Scott when I say that he wrote *Waverley*; I say of him that he is a particular individual when I say that he is the author of *Waverley*.

Although the particular proposition of identity that has been discussed is one in which the grammatical subject is a name and

---

[1] What makes a phrase a 'referring expression' is the intention of the speaker or writer. Words cannot refer, in the sense in which I am using the word, unbeknownst to the speaker. It would not then be intelligible that one should answer to the question, "To whom are you referring when you assert 'Scott was lame'"?, "I have no idea". So long as this is recognised, it could not be argued, after new discoveries had been made in nineteenth-century literary history, that it turned out that the reference of 'the author of *Waverley*', in this sentence, was not Scott, after all, but Byron.

the predicate 'is' and a definite description, we must recognise that such propositions can be expressed in sentences of which subjects and predicates can be either names or definite descriptions. Thus the following sentences can all express propositions of identity:

> "Scott was the author of *Waverley*"
> "The owner of Abbotsford was the author of *Waverley*"
> "Scott was Sir Walter"
> "The author of *Waverley* was Scott"

Of these sentences the following propositions seem to be true:

1. The logical subject may be expressed by either the grammatical subject or the grammatical predicate.
2. In each sentence the function of either the subject-phrase or the predicate-phrase, but not of both, is to refer.
3. In those sentences in which the expression other than the grammatical subject is a name it does not function as a name but as an abbreviated description.

It has often been noticed by logicians that in certain cases we can determine which part of a sentence expresses or denotes the logical subject only if we already know to what questions the proposition asserted is to be thought of as the answer. Thus, if "That building over there is the Bodleian" is the answer to the question, "What is (*or* what is the name of) that building over there?", the logical subject is 'that building over there', but if it is the answer to "Which building is the Bodleian?" the logical subject is 'the Bodleian'.[1] The fact then that sentences expressing identity propositions are reversible has inclined some logicians to the view that just as such propositions have no predicates, so they have no subjects either. If we accept this view we shall be bound to reject the view that has here been argued—namely that the function of one of the component phrases is to refer, and that the correct analysis of 'Scott was the author of *Waverley*' is to ascribe to Scott being the individual who wrote *Waverley*. It would be argued, presumably, that the function of the sentence is to assert that the reference of the name 'Scott' is

[1] It was not always noticed that this particular ambiguity occurs in identity propositions only and not in subject-predicate propositions. Whether we say "Diana of the Ephesians is great" or "Great is Diana of the Ephesians", one proposition is asserted, the logical subject of which is Diana.

the same as the reference of the phrase 'the author of *Waverley*'. But this is hard to accept. I might know that the word *mensa* and the word *Tisch* were used to refer to objects of the same kind, but I could still be ignorant of the fact that *mensa* and *Tisch* were words for 'table'. When I learn that Scott was the author of *Waverley*, I am not learning simply that a name and a definite description have the same reference. Of course, if Scott was the author of *Waverley*, then 'Scott' and 'the author of *Waverley*' *do* have the same reference, but that is because Scott alone wrote *Waverley*—that is to say, because of a fact of history not a fact about the uses of language. What may give some plausibility to this account is the fact that the name 'Scott' cannot be excluded from any formulation of the proposition. To speak of Scott is to speak of the man named 'Scott'. But the same point can be made if we consider instead such a proposition as 'The man in the armchair is the man I met yesterday'. To recognise the truth of this proposition (supposing it to be true) is not simply to recognise that the reference of the words 'The man in the armchair' and 'The man I met yesterday' is the same.

Although it is natural to assume that the grammatical subject of a sentence denotes the logical subject of the proposition expressed, this, as we have seen, is not always a correct assumption. Thus it is not possible to tell from the form of the sentence "Scott was the author of *Waverley*" if it is the name 'Scott' or the phrase 'the author of *Waverley*' which has the function of referring. But it is clear that, when the referring expression is 'the author of *Waverley*', what is asserted is that he was the individual called 'Scott'. Thus the function of the phrase 'is Scott' in such a context is, like the phrase 'is the owner of Abbotsford', singularly descriptive. Thus "Scott was Sir Walter" expresses the proposition 'Scott was the man who was called 'Sir Walter''.[1] Similarly, "My neighbour's name is Smith" expresses the proposition 'The name of my neighbour is the name 'Smith''. In their second occurrence the words 'the name' seem redundant, since it is clear that I could only intelligibly identify

[1] I have not maintained consistency in the use of inverted commas with proper names; and I do not think that there are rigid rules for their use. We normally write "'George' is his name" but "His name is George" and not "His name is 'George'". Thus, where the name 'George' is mentioned it sometimes prevents confusion to enclose it in inverted commas, but this is not always necessary.

my neighbour's name as an individual name, and not, for example, as an individual *man*.

It will have been noticed that, to all propositions in which some person or thing is asserted to be a particular individual, corresponding but not equivalent propositions can be constructed that are predicative; thus to 'The author of *Waverley* was Scott' corresponds 'The author of *Waverley* was called Scott'. The second proposition tells us less than the first; it tells us not what individual the author of *Waverley* was but one of his characteristics or attributes, namely that of being called 'Scott'.

At the best, this brief and incomplete attempt to distinguish existential, predicative and identity propositions will provoke further enquiry. Many difficulties have been left untouched and no finality is claimed for the conclusions that have been drawn. It is intended as an introduction, rather than an answer, to the problems of propositional analysis.

The notation of the calculus of predicates

The formal analyses of general propositions which we have been considering are reflected in the notation and the formulae of the *calculus of predicates* (or *predicative calculus*). This is the version of the logic of terms that was given by Russell and Whitehead in *Principia Mathematica*. Just as it may be claimed that the new analyses of general propositions which we have considered supersede the analyses of traditional logic, so, it is commonly maintained, the calculus of predicates, which takes over those new analyses, supersedes the traditional logic of the syllogism.

The laws of the predicative calculus are of two kinds; 1. those that are peculiar to itself (i.e. to the logic of terms) and 2. those that are analogues or specifications of the laws of the propositional calculus. The propositional calculus and the predicative calculus belong to one system.

The components out of which the formulae of the calculus are constructed are propositional functions, and, in Russell's view, there are, in the last analysis, only two things that can be done with a propositional function; one is to assert that it is true in *all* cases, the other to assert that it is true in at least one case, or in *some* cases. This contention may seem open to question. Surely, we may say, there is one other thing that we can do to a propositional function; we can substitute the name of an individual for 'x' in such a function as 'x is mortal', or, if the function is of the form 'fx' (where 'f' stands for any predicate whatsoever), we can substitute some particular predicate for 'f' (e.g. 'is mortal'). But logic is not concerned with individual propositions, which are contingently true or false, but with formal logical laws, laws which hold for propositions of different forms irrespective of their content. Logical laws can be exemplified by concrete arguments, but such exemplifications are not part of formal logic. Secondly, propositions about individuals have, for Russell, no place in logic for 'it is part of the definition of logic that all its propositions are completely general'. There is, then, a close parallelism between the Aristotelian logic of terms and the calculus of predicates. Both investigate systematically the logic of general propositions (whether universal or particular), not of singular propositions.

Simple propositional functions are expressed thus: 'ϕx', 'ψx', or, if English letters are used, 'fx', 'gx'. The first letter, called a *predicate variable*, stands for any predicate whatever; the second letter, the *individual variable*, should be thought of as performing the same function as the indefinite 'it' of ordinary speech and can be read either as 'it' or 'x'

To express the fact that a propositional function is true in *all* cases or in *some* cases (or, rather, at least one case), two devices are used, which are called *quantifiers*. By means of a *quantifier*, we 'quantify' or generalise the propositional function to which it is attached, its scope being indicated where necessary by brackets.

'(x)' is the Universal quantifier and is to be read 'For all x'.

'$(\exists x)$' is the Existential quantifier and is to be read 'There is an x'.

The formula '$(x)fx$' is to be read "For all x, x is f" or "Whatever x may be, it is f" or "Everything is f".

The formula $(\exists x)fx$ is to be read "There is at least one x, such that it is f" or "Something is f" or, roughly, "There are f's".

If we give a determinate value, say 'is human', for 'f' in each

of these two formulae, propositions result of which the first is false
(for not everything is human) and the second true.

A more complex example reminds us of the fact that laws of this
calculus belong to the same system of logic as the calculus of
elementary propositions. '$(x)(fx \supset gx)$', 'For all x, if it is f, it is g' or
'All f things are g', is the analogue of the A proposition of traditional
logic. The analogue of the I proposition of traditional logic is
'$(\exists x)(fx \cdot gx)$'. As we should expect, 'well-formed formulae' can
comprise symbols belonging to both notations; e.g. '$(x)(fx \supset gx) \cdot p$'.

Just as the propositional calculus can be presented as a deductive
system, so too can the calculus of predicates. The primitive ideas
peculiar to it are four in number; namely, those of the individual-
variable 'x', 'y', etc., the predicate-variable, 'f', 'g', etc., the
universal quantifier '(x)' and the existential quantifier '$(\exists x)$'.

Next, definitions of the negations of the formulae, '$(x)fx$' and
'$(\exists x)fx$', make explicit the fact that it is possible to dispense with
either one of the quantifiers.[1] Thus

$$\sim (x)fx = (\exists x) \sim fx \quad \text{Df.}$$
$$\sim (\exists x)fx = (x) \sim fx \quad \text{Df.}$$

If it is false that everything is 'f', then it must be true that there is an
'x' which is not 'f': if it is false that there is an 'x' that is 'f', then,
whatever 'x' may be, 'x' is not 'f' (*or* nothing is 'f').

I shall not quote the further eight definitions of the constants
other than negation, which the authors of *Principia Mathematica*
thought to be necessary. Nor shall I list the equivalences holding
between formulae expressed, the one set in terms of the universal
quantifier, the other in terms of the existential quantifier. It is clear,
for example, that, given the first definition above, '$(x)fx$' will be
equivalent to ' $\sim (\exists x) \sim fx$'.

As has already been said, the laws of the calculus are of two
kinds, namely those that are analogues of the laws of the
propositional calculus and those that are peculiar to itself.

That the laws of propositional logic hold for propositional
functions would seem to require no proof. If '$p \supset p$' is a law that

---

[1] Briefer positive definitions are
$$(x) = \sim (\exists x) \sim \quad \text{Df.}$$
$$(\exists x) = \sim (x) \sim \quad \text{Df.}$$

holds for any proposition whatever, then if '$(x)fx$' is the form of a proposition, '$(x)fx \supset (x)fx$' will be a specification of the law. As for the laws that are peculiar to the calculus and have no analogues in the propositional calculus, six are selected as primitive propositions in *Principia Mathematica* and these, together with the laws of the propositional calculus, constitute the axioms from which the remaining laws of the logic of predicates are derived as theorems.

Three of the most important of the laws of the calculus, the first of which is a primitive proposition while the second and the third are theorems, are

1. $(x)fx \supset (\exists x)fx$,

which may be read, "If everything is f, then there is something which is f";

2. $(r)(fx \supset gx) \supset ((x)fx \supset (x)gx)$,

which may be read, "If what is f is g, then if everything is f, everything is g";

3. $(x)(fx \cdot gx) \equiv (x)fx \cdot (x)gx$,

which may be read, "Everything is f and g if, and only if, everything is f and everything is g".

The first of these laws states the conditions under which we may validly pass from 'All' to 'Some'. It is important to notice that it does not entitle us to pass from a universal proposition (A) to a particular proposition (I). '$(x)(fx \supset gx) \supset (\exists x)(fx \supset gx)$' is an application of the law, but the form of an I proposition is not '$(\exists x)(fx \supset gx)$' ('There is an x such that if it is f, it is g'), but '$(\exists x)(fx \cdot gx)$' ('There is an x such that it is f and g'). ~But cf p 67 and p 98~

The use of the second and third laws may be illustrated in the derivation (proof) of the law

$$\{(x)(fx \supset gx) \cdot (x)(gx \supset hx)\} \supset (r)(fx \supset hx)$$

which is easily recognisable as the analogue in the calculus of the syllogistic mood Barbara

'If all M is P, and all S is M, then all S is P'

We start from the law of the propositional calculus

$$((p \supset q) \cdot (q \supset r)) \supset (p \supset r)$$

We replace p, q, r by the functions fx, gx, hx respectively. Thus we have

$$((fx \supset gx) \cdot (gx \supset hx)) \supset (fx \supset hx)$$

4+

But since this is a formal law it holds, whatever 'x' may be; so we may generalise thus

$$(x)\{[(fx \supset gx) \cdot (gx \supset hx)] \supset (fx \supset hx)\}$$

Now we can regard the whole expression that follows the quantifier '(x)' as a compound material implication; so we can derive from this law, in accordance with the second law quoted above, namely '$(x)(fx\supset gx)\supset[(x)fx\supset(x)gx)]$', the law

1. $(x)[(fx\supset gx)\cdot(gx\supset hx)]\supset(x)(fx\supset hx)$

Next, since in accordance with the third law above, viz. '$(x)(fx\cdot gx)\equiv(x)fx\cdot(x)gx$', the whole expression in 1, which precedes the main constant '$\supset$', is materially equivalent to

$$(x)(fx \supset gx) \cdot (x)(gx \supset hx),$$

we can derive from 1. the law,

$$[(x)(fx \supset gx) \cdot (x)(gx \supset hx)] \supset (x)(fx \supset hx),$$

which is the law which we set out to prove.

The purpose of this very brief account of the calculus of predicates has been to introduce the elements of the notation and show how it is related to the calculus of propositions as part of the same deductive system. If we are to accept it as providing a satisfactory analysis of the logic of terms we must be satisfied on two general counts; first, that the analysis of propositions which it gives is correct or at least is to be preferred to the Aristotelian analysis; second, that the constants of the propositional calculus, which, as we have seen, are taken over into the notation of the calculus of predicates, adequately represent those propositional links in virtue of which propositions stand in relations of logical necessity to one another.

In the earlier part of this chapter I ignored any differences that there may be between '$p\supset q$' and 'if p, q' and represented the new analysis of universal propositions as 'Whatever x may be, if x is f, it is g'. But since, in the notation of the calculus, this is the formula '$(x)(fx\supset gx)$', such an interpretation is open to the same criticisms as were considered earlier, when the propositional calculus was under discussion. Mr Strawson has drawn attention to the fact that, if we accept '$\sim(\exists x)(fx\cdot\sim gx)$' as an analysis of the proposition, 'All the books in his room are by English authors', we must admit that the proposition is true if, in fact, there are no books in his room at all, since '$\sim(\exists x)(fx) \supset \sim(\exists x)(fx \cdot \sim gx)$' is a law.[1] If we find this consequence unacceptable and therefore raise objections to the analysis, it is important that we should recognise that the ground for our criticism is not a peculiarity of the predicate calculus, but is to be located further back in the rules for the logical constants.

As for the question whether the analysis of propositions which the calculus provides is acceptable, we must recognise how far-reaching are the claims made on its behalf. Quantificational analysis is offered not only for propositions which are expressed in sentences the subjects of which include the words 'all' and 'some'. Propositions expressed in sentences the subjects of which are indefinite and definite descriptions are also analysed in the same way. I have argued that the analysis is appropriate and revealing when indefinite descriptions are involved and in some of the cases in which definite descriptions are used. But I have also argued that some sentences of which the grammatical subjects are definite descriptions are not existential and that therefore to represent them by quantified formulae is to some extent to distort them. But it has not been argued that the quantificational analysis of such propositions results in the misrepresentation of general logical laws. If it is objectionable, it is because it suggests that definite descriptions cannot be used, as proper names can be used, to express the logical subjects of subject-predicate propositions.

Logical notations

We have now, briefly, reviewed three logical notations: those of traditional logic, of the propositional calculus and of the predicative calculus. The second and third of these not only enable us to express logical relations more perspicuously but give us a deeper understanding of the structure of propositions. It may then be reasonably asked why the vocabulary of traditional logic has not been abandoned entirely, at least by those logicians who regard modern logic as superseding traditional logic. In fact, few logicians exclude altogether from their discussion such formulae as 'All S is P' and 'Some S is P'.

There are perhaps three chief reasons for the survival of the traditional notation; the first is the fact that in it the forms of

[1] P. F. Strawson, *op. cit.*, ch. 5, pt. II.

propositions bear close analogies to the forms of common speech; the second, that after many centuries of philosophical writing it has become familiar to us. Only after a student has familiarised himself with the notation of the predicative calculus by continual practice and study is he likely to find the formulae for the forms of syllogisms as *natural* as those of the older text-books. But there is a further reason why we are often inclined to retain the older notation. Although, as I have tried to show, the form of an argument cannot be defined as that in virtue of which the argument is valid, we are generally concerned with the formal features of propositions only in so far as they are relevant to displaying the logical relations in which they stand in a given context. Thus we tend to adopt in discussion the simplest formulae which reveal the logic of an argument, even if those formulae lack precision. The formal differences between universal and singular propositions may sometimes be ignored and their formal similarities emphasised. Consider the dialogue:

> "Whoever said that was misinformed"
> "John was the man who told me"
> "In that case, somebody has misled him"

The second sentence expresses a singular proposition of identity, but to represent it as of subject-predicate form and the whole dialogue as an instance of a traditional syllogism in Barbara, 'All M is P, (All) S is M, therefore (All) S is P', seems in some contexts an excusable distortion. But there is a price to pay for the assimilation of complex arguments to the simple forms of traditional logic. Their attractive simplicity and their close resemblance to standard grammatical forms provided logicians with no incentive to attempt more penetrating analyses. It is not surprising that all, or almost all, the major advances in logical theory and analysis during the last century and a half have been made by philosophers with a mathematical and not a philological background.

5

PROPOSITIONS AND FACTS

Wordsworth is reported to have said that language is not the clothing but the incarnation of thought. Are we justified in rejecting this view that the words and sentences which we utter are themselves our thoughts and not merely the means by which, or the medium in which, we express them? Certainly there seem to be good reasons for maintaining it.

When I recognise that the grass needs cutting, the thought seems to take shape in the very words that I use to express it. Though we are sometimes inclined to say that we cannot find words adequate to express our thoughts, reflection on such situations often seems to point to the conclusion that, until we find words to express a particular thought, the thought itself is vague and indeterminate. It is certainly misleading to think of language in general as a tool or instrument, at any rate when the purpose of our speech is to express that which we claim to be true. I choose one tool rather than another to achieve a particular result; for example, I use a fork, it may be, rather than a spade to dig my garden. It would be misleading to describe as a tool anything the operation of which is not a matter of choice or selection on my part. Thus, although I may select one medium of communication rather than another, in that I may decide to express myself in writing rather than orally, and although I may choose one word in preference to another, it is not the case that I decide to use 'language-in-general' to express my thoughts. Thought realises itself, is actualised, only in language.

But these considerations should not lead us to abandon the distinction that has been drawn between sentences and propositions. Wordsworth no doubt had poetry in mind when he made the observation which I have quoted. A poem is not the sense or purport of the lines that the poet writes or recites; rather it is thought and feeling *as expressed in* certain particular words and sentences and no others. A paraphrase of a poem is not the poem itself, and there is no such thing as a 'poem in translation', if what were meant by that phrase were the same, original poem expressed in a different language; for a poem consists of determinate words and phrases. But it is clear that for some purposes the distinction between uttered words and sentences and their purport or 'substance' is permissible and indeed necessary. If I am asked for the opening theme of a piano sonata, I must play, sing or whistle the actual notes; if I am asked for the opening lines of Hamlet, I must quote the words that Shakespeare wrote; but if I am asked what instructions I have received or what information I have been given, I can report without quoting. I take it as axiomatic that though men think and speak in different languages, they may still consider the same problems and ask the same questions. Thus while propositions can be expressed only in words, they are not the words in which they are expressed. The same proposition can be expressed in an indefinitely large number of different sentences in the same language or different languages.[1]

The proposition that a sentence is used to express is, in one clearly recognisable sense of the word 'meaning', the meaning of the sentence. And since the word 'meaning' is used in different senses, we must be clear which sense this is.

A proposition is a particular thought that a speaker seeks to convey to his hearers, it is a meaning in the sense that it is what he, the speaker, means. Different speakers at different times and in different circumstances may use the same sentence to express different propositions or, in the sense of the word 'meaning' with which we are here concerned, different meanings. Thus a man in the seventeenth century might report the death of Charles I in the same words in which a man sixty-six years later might report the death of Louis XIV. Each might say, "The King is dead", but they would be seek-

---

[1] The function of expressing propositions, which can be true or false, is almost certainly not the commonest function of speech, but it is the function with which the logician is particularly concerned. So when I speak of the proposition that a particular sentence is used to express, I do not wish to suggest that all grammatical sentences express propositions.

ing to convey different propositions, different meanings, that is to say, different things meant. So, in the sense of 'meaning' in which a meaning is that which a speaker uttering a sentence conveys or attempts to convey, propositions are meanings.

But it is easy to confuse this sense with another. Perhaps most commonly we mean by the word 'meaning', not what a given speaker meant on a given occasion, but what we are inclined to say 'the sentence itself means'. In this sense of the word 'meaning', to know what the sentence, "The King is dead", means is not to know what particular piece of information a particular speaker was intending to convey, but what is common to all the 'things meant' by the sentence, on different occasions of its use, when it is used 'correctly', i.e. in accordance with the standard rules of usage. In other words, by 'meaning' in this sense we mean the highest common factor of all the meanings, in the *first* sense of 'meaning', which speakers of a language seek to convey when they are speaking correctly.[1]

Let us call this second sense of meaning 'general meaning' and the first sense, 'thing meant'. Clearly it is possible to know the general meaning of a sentence and not to know the thing meant by it on a particular occasion of its use. I can know the general meaning of "The King is dead" without knowing what king a particular user of the sentence has or had in mind when he uttered it. Conversely it seems to be possible on some occasions for one to understand the thing meant by a sentence without knowing its general meaning. I might, for instance, understand that a Turkish innkeeper was telling me that he could not provide me with a meal without knowing the general meaning of the sentence that he used to convey the information.

Propositions, then, are the things meant by particular sentences. Yet they can be general meanings also, namely in those cases where the thing meant *is* a general meaning, where what a particular speaker in a particular context wishes to convey is what *any* speaker in *any* context would wish to convey by the same sentence. Thus, what different speakers at different times mean by such sentences as "All men are mortal" or "Some summers are wet" is the same provided that they are speaking in accordance with standard rules of

[1] But see also p. 117.

English usage. In terms of the arithmetical simile that we used before, the highest common factor of what the sentences severally mean is the whole of what they mean.

It is not difficult to cite further examples of sentences of which the thing meant and the general meanings coincide. They will include sentences expressing all sorts of general propositions, proverbs, e.g. "A stitch in time saves nine", and historical statements which are contextually independent, e.g. "William of Normandy won the Battle of Hastings in A.D. 1066". On the other hand, "William of Normandy won the Battle of Hastings 895 years ago" is a sentence which can be used to express a true proposition in 1961 but a false (and *different*) proposition in any other year.

We may perhaps understand better what sort of things propositions are or, at least, what they are not, if we consider the form in which they are commonly expressed; namely in noun-clauses beginning with the word 'that'. Thus, if John said "The dog is asleep", we should say that the proposition which he asserted was that the dog was asleep. Now what is the function of the word 'that' in the noun-clause, "that the dog was asleep"? Is it simply a stylistic variant of inverted commas? In that case,

"John said that the dog was asleep"
is synonymous with

"John said "The dog is asleep" "
If we interpret the function of 'that' in this way, the proposition, 'that the dog was asleep', turns out to be merely a collection of words like the quoted sentence "The dog is asleep". We should then conclude that propositions are after all merely words.

But this account of the function of 'that' is unsatisfactory. For in the sentence, "John said "The dog is asleep" ", I *report* John's utterance; in the sentence, "John said that the dog was asleep", I do not report what he said but *interpret* it. The two sentences do not have the same function, and if I were to say "When John said "the dog is asleep" he asserted that the dog was asleep", I should not be merely repeating myself. Of course it would be absurd to say such a thing as this because, if the quoted sentence were not understood, the interpretation, which is expressed in the same words, would not be understood either. But logically the sentence is parallel to "When Macaulay, as a child, said "The agony is abated", he meant that he was in less pain". And no one would be tempted to describe *this* sentence as merely repetitive or tautologous.

We should distinguish between such sentences as

1. " "Le roi est mort" means the same as "Der König ist tot" "
and

2. " "Le roi est mort" means that the King is dead".

2. gives either the general meaning of, or the 'thing meant' by, the quoted sentence; 1. does not give the meaning at all. What constantly tempts us to think of propositions as combinations of words is the fact that they can only be expressed *in* words. The proposition which a sentence is used to express is, not another sentence, but that which it is logically possible to think to be the case and which, when the sentence is actually used to make a statement, *is* thought to be the case.

Statements and propositions

It is a common practice among logicians to use the word 'statement' instead of 'proposition' to name those entities between which logical relations hold. At this stage it seems appropriate that I should attempt to justify my preference for the word 'proposition'.

Propositions are asserted or denied, considered, accepted and posed. When I ask "Did Cromwell die in 1658?" I pose a proposition for your consideration. You may after investigation accept the proposition as true; that is to say, accept it as true that Cromwell died in 1658. You may express your acceptance of it as true by asserting it in the indicative sentence, "Cromwell died in 1658". We can, then, distinguish entertaining or considering propositions from accepting them as true (or rejecting them as false) and from asserting or denying them.[1] But logic is not concerned with what we 'do to' or 'do about' propositions. Though I cannot recognise the implications of a proposition without entertaining it, it is the proposition entertained, not my entertaining the proposition, that implies (or does not imply) further propositions. In the same way, the fact that the proposition that no mammals are invertebrates implies that no invertebrates are mammals is not dependent on my asserting one or

[1] On propositions ('thoughts') generally, see G. Frege, *The Thought: a logical enquiry*, tr. Quinton, *Mind*, 1956.

4*

other of these propositions. We do not create logical relations between propositions by stating them, and if we are to avoid confusing psychology with logic, we should keep distinct the asserting of a proposition from the proposition itself. The use of the word 'statement' encourages us to blur this distinction; for statements, in the usual sense of the word, exist in being stated or asserted. Moreover, if, in our logical vocabulary, we replace 'proposition' by 'statement', we are in danger of thinking of logic as primarily concerned with the appraisal of the logic of men's arguments and assertions. We appraise our own or other people's performances, but this is not the logician's primary function. He is concerned primarily with the elucidation of the principles of true implication, not with the success or failure of men's attempts to state and argue in accordance with them.

The view that logical relations hold between statements is incompatible with the assumption (which, so far as I know, no logician is tempted to deny) that a single series of propositional variables, 'p', 'q', 'r' etc., can be used to represent the constituents of both simple and compound propositions. As we have seen, it is standard practice to represent hypothetical propositions as 'if p, q', 'if p, then q', '$p \supset q$', and to use the same letters, 'p', 'q' and 'r', to represent simple (or, rather, unanalysed) propositions. But only if 'p', 'q' and 'r' represent the forms of propositions, and not the forms of statements, can they be interpreted unequivocally. The clauses of conditional sentences do not express statements; when I say "If it rains, the match will be cancelled", I do not state that it will rain or that the match will be cancelled. But both the sentence, "It will rain", and the clause "If it rains", present us with the same thought, namely the thought that it will rain, asserted in the one case and entertained or supposed in the other. It is with the meaning or content which is common to both that the logician is concerned and which, *because* it is the same in both cases, he unequivocally symbolises as 'p'.

In spite of these objections to the replacement of the word 'proposition' by 'statement' in logical discussions, it is intelligible that they should not at first strike one. The most natural way of presenting a proposition for consideration is to use an indicative sentence—"The cat is on the mat", "The King is dead", "It will rain"—and one may easily fail to notice that sentences in the indicative have a double function. What this is, is clearly pointed out by Frege. "Two things", he says, "must be distinguished in an indicative sentence: the content, which it has in common with the corresponding sentence-question, and the assertion." As he goes on to say, "both are so closely joined in an indicative sentence that it is easy to overlook their separability".[1] It is above all because the use of the word 'statement' as a substitute for 'proposition' tends to hide from us this vital distinction between what is logically relevant and what is logically irrelevant, that it is safest to exclude it as far as possible from logical discussions.

I do not wish to suggest that the current preference for the word 'statement' is to be explained as arising from mistakes in analysis or a confusion between logic and psychology. The philosophers in whose works this preference is most clearly revealed are empiricists and as such are reluctant to admit the reality of non-empirical objects. It is easier to maintain that statements are empirical objects than that propositions are. Propositions, if there are such things, are entities which are non-sensible and non-linguistic. On the other hand, we do not think of statements as things that need to be sharply distinguished from words and sounds, which can be seen or heard. We should not be surprised, then, when we find that empiricist logicians not only prefer 'statement' to 'proposition' but also play down the 'sentence-statement' distinction.

Indeed, it has been argued that to adopt a vocabulary which minimises the distinction between sentences and propositions has positive philosophical advantages. Mr Strawson prefers, as the formulation of a proposition of logical necessity, "The statement that he is over six feet tall entails the statement that he is not under six feet tall" (which, of course, easily lends itself to the abbreviation, " "He is over six feet tall" entails "He is not under six feet tall" ") to the formulation, "He cannot be both over and under six feet tall". For him the error (if, after all, it is an error) of thinking of entailment as holding between sentences, to which adoption of his preferred formulation may incline us, is less serious than that of confusing logical with causal necessity, which is the danger that we run if we adopt the latter formulation.

[1] Frege, *op. cit.*

But this, I suspect, is not the whole story. It is not a coincidence that some of the logicians who favour the displacement of the traditional 'proposition' by 'statement' advocate a theory of logic in accordance with which logic is derivable from rules of language. The plausibility of this theory, which will be considered in the next chapter, is increased by every step in the argument which narrows the gap between propositions of logic and grammatical sentences. When we replace 'proposition' by 'statement', we take such a step. From the point of view of the theorists in question, it is a step in the right direction.

The question, "What are the entities between which logical relations hold?", or, to put it more simply, "What sorts of thing can fill the gaps in "—— implies ——"?", seems to be, not a question of metaphysics, but, in a wide sense of the word, of experience. More precisely it seems to be a question that we can answer by considering the evidence of ordinary language, by asking ourselves what we *say* and by reflecting on what we *mean* by what we say. What sorts of expression do we, in our ordinary speech, use in place of the dashes in sentences of the form "—— implies ——"? When we ask ourselves this question, it may come as something of a shock to recognise the remoteness of some common formulations of propositions of implication from those of ordinary speech.

No one except a logical theorist would be tempted to say that such-and-such a statement implies (or entails) such-and-such another statement; for example, "The statement that he is over six feet tall entails the statement that he is under six feet tall". But it may be objected that it is proper for logicians to invent a technical vocabulary of clearly defined terms. We do not in ordinary life say that statements imply statements but nor do we say that propositions imply propositions. But this objection can be met: the word statement is a word of common language and it has not been redefined or given a new meaning as a technical term of logic. Thus the claim that statements imply statements is a claim that the word 'statement' in its ordinary sense is the correct word to apply to those entities which we would say imply one another. And this is false. For it to be acceptable it is necessary that the word should be given a new and technical meaning.

The case is different with the word 'proposition'. This is a technical term which has no exact synonym in everyday language. By it is intended that which can be thought to be the case, that which is the content or 'sense' of sentences and clauses and which is true or false. So if we maintain that propositions imply propositions, we make a claim that cannot be directly verified or falsified by appeal to ordinary language. We must verify it *indirectly* by satisfying ourselves that the phrases linked by such words as 'imply' and 'entail' in our ordinary speech express what we have decided to call propositions.

Facts

The answer to the question, "What sorts of things imply and are implied?", to which unbiased consideration of ordinary usage leads us, is a surprising one. It is that *facts* imply. Indeed we seldom use the word 'imply' unqualified except when that which is said to imply either is called a fact or could be re-expressed as a fact. Of course it is not necessary that in expressing propositions of logical necessity we should use the word 'imply' or 'entail' at all. Thus we may say "Since all men are mortal and Socrates is a man, Socrates is mortal"; but if we express ourselves in a sentence in which the word 'imply' occurs, we find that we most naturally say "The fact that all men are mortal and that Socrates is a man implies that Socrates is mortal". It is true that we can also say "That all men are mortal and that Socrates is a man etc.", but when we do so we should, I think, be prepared to agree that this formulation is an abbreviation of the former and that the phrase "That all men etc." is to be understood as "The fact that all men etc." We interpret other formulations of the premisses of statements of implication, in which the actual word 'fact' does not occur, in the same way. Thus, 'His silence implies consent' is to be interpreted as 'The fact that he is silent implies that he consents'.

It is true that we also use the word 'imply' in cases where we do not commit ourselves to the truth of the premisses. So instead of saying, 'If Marxists are materialists, and if Tom is a Marxist, he must be a materialist', we may say something like "the supposition that Marxists are materialists and that Tom is a Marxist would imply that he is a materialist". But here we assert, not that an implication holds, but that it *would* hold if certain propositions were true. It would seem that it is facts, above all, that unqualifiedly imply.

That facts imply is a conclusion that has appeared altogether unacceptable to many philosophers. It is not difficult to see why. The world, it is thought, consists of facts; they constitute the actual. But if to say this is to say that facts are events, states of affairs, the constituents of the physical universe, the conclusion that facts imply must surely be mistaken. One would wish to argue that events and states of affairs stand in *causal*, but not *logical*, relations with other events and states of affairs. To say that physical events conform to logical laws would be to assimilate the laws of logic to the laws of physics. But neither physicists nor logicians have been tempted to include the principles of syllogism in a list of physical laws. This difficulty will disappear only if we can show that the identification of facts with events and states of affairs is mistaken.

Let us assume that a man named John Smith drove his car into the back of a stationary lorry when he was drunk. On this assumption, it is a fact that John Smith was drunk when the accident occurred. At the same time it is a fact that the driver of the car was drunk when the accident occurred. Should we wish to say that we are here presented with one fact or with two? If with one, then it would seem to follow that if we knew that the driver of the car was drunk, we should also know that John Smith was drunk, for *ex hypothesi* there is only one fact to be known. But this is false. Clearly it is possible that I should know that the driver was drunk without knowing his name, and equally possible that I should know that John Smith was drunk without knowing that he was the driver of a car involved in an accident. Moreover, to know that the driver of a car was drunk clearly is to know a fact. So we are led to the conclusion that the two noun-clauses express not one fact but two.

But surely, if we are here presented with two facts, they are facts about one individual man? There was only one man who was drunk and was involved in the accident. If the fact that the driver was drunk is different from the fact that John Smith was drunk, the difference must lie in this—that whereas one fact is about the driver of the car, the other is about John Smith. For in every other respect the facts are identical. Yet the man that was drunk *was* John Smith.

Should we then conclude that after all we are only concerned with one fact—the fact, about one and the same man, that he was drunk? The answer is that the subject of each fact is different although only one man is involved. The subject of the first fact is one particular man *as thought of as* the driver of the car; the subject of the other is the same man *as thought of as* the man who is named John Smith.

Would it be possible, in this context, to replace the clumsy phrase, 'as thought of as', by 'as described as'? No, because the criterion for identifying the subject is not that the English words, 'driver of the car', are applicable to the subject, but that whatever words are used to designate it (whether in English, French or any other language) should mean what the words 'driver of the car' mean. Even the phrase 'as thought of as' does not quite convey the required shade of meaning. If it is a fact that the driver of the car was drunk, then it is a fact whether or not anyone knows it to be such; and to speak of the subject of a fact as *thought* of in a particular way might suggest that the fact has been acknowledged by someone, i.e. by whoever *has thought* of the subject in that way. Strictly, then, by 'as thought of as' I mean 'as a possible object of thought as'. At the same time, however, we should notice that the different fact, that John Smith was drunk, is a fact about a subject who is identifiable not by a description, which could be expressed in an indefinite number of different ways, but as being the bearer of a particular proper name (which consists of the two words, 'John' and 'Smith', and no others). Hence it is a fact about a man as *named* John Smith. To know this fact it would be necessary to know the *name* of its subject.

To argue that facts imply does not commit us to the implausible view that logical laws are the most basic of physical laws; for facts are not events, states of affairs or physical constituents of the universe, and it is with these that physics is concerned. Our supposed traffic accident is not a fact; what *is* a fact is (we are assuming) *that the traffic accident occurred*. The battle of Waterloo is an *event* in British history: that a battle was fought at Waterloo is a fact. The battle occurred nearly a century and a half ago. It is over and done with. But it *is* a fact that the battle occurred at that time. Thus events have their places in time but facts do not. They are timeless as the truth of propositions is timeless. No one is tempted to say that negative or hypothetical events occur, but there are both negative and hypothetical facts. It is a fact that Socrates did not die in battle, and perhaps it is a fact that if Hannibal had marched on Rome after Cannae he would have taken it.

What then are facts? We have seen that they are not to be identified with events or physical states, and that for every event there is not one (and only one) corresponding fact; they stand in logical relations to one another; they are timeless; they can be negative or hypothetical. All these things we can say, too, of propositions and for the same reasons; for facts *are* propositions, not all propositions, but those that are true. It is not surprising, then, that we can always substitute the phrase 'It is true' for 'It is a fact'. It is a fact (or it is true) that a battle was fought at Waterloo; it is a fact (or it is true) that Socrates did not die in battle. Perhaps we feel some uneasiness about saying that it may be a *fact* that if Hannibal had marched on Rome after Cannae he would have taken it, but it is the same uneasiness that we feel about saying that it may be *true* that if he had marched on Rome he would have taken it. The true proposition that Socrates died by drinking hemlock is a proposition about Socrates. Equally we may say that the fact that Socrates so died is a *fact* about Socrates.

A brief excursion into the 'theory of knowledge', that is to say the philosophical investigation of the extent to which we can have knowledge of the world, may help to make this view of the status of facts more readily acceptable. Empirical statements are those the truth or falsity of which we can establish by observation and experiment, the senses providing us with the data by reference to which they are checked. This checking-procedure we may naturally describe as one of *comparing* the statements made with the data that the senses provide. We tend to assume, too, that this evidence is provided by the senses pure and uninterpreted. Thus, on this view, we have, on the one hand, the statement to be checked and, on the other, the uninterpreted evidence 'given' to us in perception. But, if we consider the procedure of verifying an individual empirical statement, we shall see that this account is over-simplified.

Assume that it has been asserted that there is an armchair in the room next to that in which I am sitting. I verify the assertion by going into the next room and seeing if, in fact, there is an armchair there. But how exactly do I verify it and with what do I compare my original assertion?

First of all it must be agreed that it is not enough that a chair should lie within my field of vision; it is also necessary that I should *notice* the chair, that I should see that there is a chair there. It may be that a man may properly be said to see something if that thing lies in his field of vision, if his eyes are open and he has good sight, if he is not asleep or in a trance, even though he is unconscious of the thing which he is said to see. But it is clear that, if I saw only in that minimal sense of the word 'see', I should not be in possession of the data that I need to verify the original assertion. Only if I am consciously aware of a chair have I the knowledge that entitles me to say that the statement was true; only if I see that there is no chair in the room, am I entitled to say that the statement was false. But to see that there is not a chair in the room, perhaps more obviously than seeing that there *is* a chair there, is not a case of the purely passive reception of visual stimuli.

The lesson that I wish to draw from this illustration is that we cannot get *behind* propositions to a 'non-propositionally-given' world, to a world of empirical data for the apprehension of which I need sense-organs but no thought or intelligence. For us to become aware of the world we must 'factualise' or 'propositionalise' it. So when I check the original assertion, "There is a chair in the next room", I compare it not with uninterpreted presentations of sense, but with *another proposition*. This second proposition has greater authority in that it is one that is formulated when I am actually observing the subject of the assertion; but it is a proposition none the less. Facts are events and states of affairs (or, quite generally, what is the case) *as they can be thought about and recognised by us.*

The error of assuming that there is a non-propositionally given world, with which we can compare propositions, is a defect of most versions of a well-known theory about the nature of truth, the so-called 'Correspondence Theory'. Its supporters hold that truth (at least so far as it is applicable to empirical propositions) consists of the correspondence or agreement of propositions with facts. They hold, too, that propositions and facts are different in kind. But if the account of facts that has here been given is sound, the theory is mistaken or, at the best, vacuously uninformative.

Let us see how this is so. According to the theory, the proposition, 'There is a chair in the next room', is true if it corresponds with the facts. But what facts? Clearly there is only one fact that is relevant—the fact that there is (we may suppose) a chair in the next room. So, it seems, we are entitled to reformulate the claim thus: "For the proposition, 'There is a chair in the next room', to be true is for it to correspond with the fact that there is a chair in the next room". But this, according to my argument, is to say, "For the proposition, 'There is a chair in the next room', to be true is for it to correspond with the true proposition, 'There is a chair in the next room'". To say this seems to be to say no more than that a proposition is true if it is true. The theory seems to be particularly mistaken when it is interpreted as implying that facts are different in kind from true propositions.

In the account of facts that I have given I have appealed for support to our ordinary use of language. Yet one of the principal objections to such accounts has been, I suspect, the belief that it does *not* accord with common usage. In particular, correspondence theorists would, I think, point to the fact that in our everyday speech, as well as in philosophical arguments, we say of true statements that they 'correspond with' or 'fit' the facts. Surely it cannot be the case that when we say, for example, of the account that someone has given of his movements that it cannot be true because it does not correspond with the facts, we mean no more than that his account cannot be true because it is not true? It is implausible to suggest that a common English idiom which we at any rate *think* we use to some purpose expresses no more than a disguised tautology. To this I agree. "Your account does not correspond with the facts" does not express a tautology, but neither does it support the correspondence theory, as we may see if we consider the following imaginary situation.

John is reproaching George for failing to keep an appointment.

George: "I waited in your room between six and a quarter past, and you didn't turn up."

John: "What you say simply doesn't fit (*or* correspond with) the facts."

George: "Why do you say that?"

John: "Well, I know that you didn't leave home before six

since you yourself admitted just now that you heard the beginning of the news on the wireless, and you can't pretend that you can get here from your house in less than ten minutes."

Now if the correspondence theorist were to gain the support that he claims from common usage, he would need to show that what we mean when we say that a statement does (or does not) correspond with the facts is that the statement stands (or does not stand) in a 'one-one' relationship to 'its' fact (rather as my photograph 'corresponds' with me). He is arguing that propositions mirror or represent or picture (or fail to mirror or represent or picture) corresponding, correlative facts. But this is not what we mean when we speak thus. What we are saying is that a particular statement (e.g. George's statement that he waited between 6 and 6.15 in a particular room) is not compatible with *other* propositions that, it is assumed, are known to be true (and are therefore referred to as 'facts'). John's objection to George's account is that it is logically *inconsistent* with other propositions. The correspondence theorist who appeals for support to ordinary language has misunderstood the meaning of the words 'correspond' and 'fit' in such contexts. When we use these common idioms, we appeal, perhaps unconsciously, to the principle that if two propositions are logically inconsistent one at least must be false.[1]

It is not necessary that we should here decide how much the correspondence theory can contribute to our understanding of the nature of truth. Perhaps its only service is to remind us of what we have no temptation to doubt, that the truth of empirical propositions in some sense 'turns on' or 'depends on' actual events and states of affairs, in a way in which the truth of mathematical and logical propositions does not; in other words it may remind us of the difference between empirical and non-empirical propositions.

The identification of propositions

What criteria should we adopt for identifying propositions? Under what conditions are we entitled to say of two or more sentences that they express the same proposition? Hitherto it has

[1] Of course two propositions could be consistent but both be false. So one might say "What you say corresponds with the account that your friend gave, but I suspect that you are both lying".

been said that two sentences would express the same subject-predicate proposition if the same thing were predicated of the same subject and if the subject were, in each case, thought of in the same way. Thus "The driver of the car was drunk" and "The person who drove the car was intoxicated" express the same proposition. But the phrase 'in the same way' is vague and we must look for greater precision.

Let us first consider propositions in the expression of which such words are used as 'I', 'you', 'we', 'he', 'this', 'that', 'here', 'now', 'ago', 'today', 'yesterday', 'tomorrow'. What are we to say of 'Jones cashed a cheque on the 5th January 1959' and the proposition asserted by Jones himself on the 6th January 1959, 'I cashed a cheque yesterday'. Common sense suggests that in both cases the same proposition is asserted. At least, to establish the truth of one is to establish the truth of the other. Yet there appears to be a difficulty. In an earlier illustration, "John Smith was drunk" was said to express a different proposition than "The driver of the car was drunk", on the grounds that the subject was thought of differently in each case—in the one, as driver of the car; in the other, as bearer of the name, 'John Smith'. Are we entitled to say that 'I' and 'Jones' here designate the same subject as thought of in the same way?

Now when Jones makes a statement about himself and uses the personal pronoun, 'I', he does not refer to himself as thought of in any particular way or as bearer of a particular name. Yet in the appropriate context he would accept a reformulation of the proposition which he asserted, framed in the third person and with 'Jones' as subject. For to refer to oneself as 'I' is not to prescribe a particular way in which one is to be thought of. It would seem that the use of 'I' does not exclude any unambiguously identifying form of words provided that the appropriateness of the words is recognisable by the subject in question. Thus although "Jones cashed a cheque", "The householder who lives at 7 Acacia Road cashed a cheque" and "The city engineer of Barchester cashed a cheque" express propositions that are different from one another, provided that Jones knows his own name, address and occupation, he would have to agree that each was 'contained in' the proposition expressed by him as "I cashed a cheque".

The words listed—'I', 'you', 'here', 'ago', 'yesterday' etc.—may be said to chain propositions to the context of their assertion. We sever the chains when we re-express them in language for the understanding of which no knowledge of the original context of their assertion is needed. From the resulting reformulations all the words listed disappear except when they refer back to something within the proposition itself (e.g. the word 'he' in "Jones cashed a cheque and he overdrew his account").

It is not necessary that the verbs of sentences should be in the same tense for one and the same proposition to be expressed. Thus "Jones will cash a cheque on the 5th January" can express the same proposition as "Jones is cashing a cheque now on the 5th January" or "Jones cashed a cheque on the 5th January". Were this not so, statements about the future would not be verifiable. Of course it would be strange to say that these sentences have the same 'general meaning'; they are not interchangeable like "He mounted his steed" and "He got on his horse" or "Le roi est mort" and "The King is dead". Clearly the first sentence is appropriate only before Jones has cashed his cheque and the last only after he has done so.

Indeed, consideration of tense-differences suggests that the earlier account of 'general meaning' is over-simplified. It was then said that the 'general meaning' of a sentence was the highest common factor of the possible 'things meant' by the sentence when it is used in accordance with standard usage. But to understand the general meaning of a sentence, in the widest sense, would include understanding the conditions under which it could be used to express propositions significantly. This may lead us to include under 'general meaning' both the highest common factor of the propositions (or 'things meant') that could be expressed by a given sentence when it is used in a standard way and the conditions under which it can be used to express such propositions. In other words, we may wish to say that a man only understands the general meaning of a statement-making sentence when he understands what sort of things the sentence is used to assert and, at the same time, the general rules of language in accordance with which the sentence is constructed to express the thing meant.

The fact that the verbs which are used in the expression of propositions are tensed—in the past, present or future—raises a doubt if propositions can be considered without *some* reference to the context of their assertion. For what dictates the tense of verbs is not only the time of the events reported but also the time at which the report (or assertion) is made. Thus the sentence, "Jones cashed a cheque on 5th January", expresses a proposition in the tense appropriate to a report made after the event. Only timeless propositions (e.g. 'Salt dissolves in water', 'The internal angles of a triangle are equal to two right-angles') are expressed in a form which gives no clue to the time at which they are asserted. Language is not equipped with a 'neutral' tense in which propositions about datable events can be expressed with equal appropriateness before, at the time when, and after they occur.

When we considered the logic of elementary propositions, we noticed certain verbal differences in sentences which do not result in differences in the propositions which they are used to express. The sentences, "Mary is poor and honest" and "Although Mary is poor, she is honest", express the same proposition and differ only in that they reveal or anticipate differences in attitude on the part of speaker or audience to that which is asserted. Again, we have seen that an indefinitely large range of 'merely verbal' changes can be made in sentences without altering the proposition expressed. To deny this would amount to a denial of the possibility of expressing the same proposition in different natural languages. But it is not always easy to decide when a change in expression is merely verbal. What are we to say of "Jean is English" and "It is not the case that Jean is not English", or of "Jean is English or French" and "It is not the case that Jean is neither English nor French"?

If we say that these are pairs of synonymous sentences and that they differ only verbally, we commit ourselves to saying that '*p* implies *p*' and '*p* implies not *not-p*', on the one hand, and '*p* or *q*' and 'not (*not-p* and *not-q*)', on the other, are merely literary variants. But one cannot be happy with this conclusion. So let us see if we can formulate conditions which must be satisfied if different sentences are to express identical propositions.

First, the truth-value of the propositions expressed must be the same. Second, the elements in the proposition must be thought of in the same way not only in respect of content, but also in respect of form. Thus we may say of the propositions, 'John Smith was drunk' and 'The driver of the car was drunk', that they satisfy the first condition but not the second; in respect of *content*, the subject in each case is thought of differently. What makes 'Jean is English' a different proposition from 'It is not the case that Jean is not English' is the fact that what is propounded is thought of differently in each in respect of *form*. In a later chapter an attempt will be made to throw more light on the question of what ingredients of propositions are properly to be called formal.

6

LOGIC AND LANGUAGE: I

How do the principles of logic arise? How are we to explain the fact that formal logic consists of just those laws which we recognise as valid and not other laws? Logical laws, it is worth repeating, are not rules that we lay down for our own convenience. We do not *prescribe* that if all men are mortal and if Socrates is a man, we are to *grant* it is true that Socrates is mortal. No, we recognise that if the premisses are true, the conclusion must *be* true. Nor, on the other hand, are logical laws empirical generalisations which we are led to formulate by observation or experiment. Experience has not taught us the principle that if a proposition is true, its contradictory must be false and no experience could lead us to abandon it. In this chapter I shall consider one of the answers that has been given to this question.

The theory which I shall consider is one that can be described as 'linguistic-conventionalist', and the presentation of it to which I shall refer is that provided by Mr P. F. Strawson in his *Introduction to Logical Theory*.[1] According to this theory, the accepted principles of logic arise, in some way, out of the most general rules of language, namely the rules that determine the structure of grammatically correct utterances whatever the subject-matter or content of those utterances may be. It seems to be held that, in adopting certain kinds of expression which appear to be common to all natural languages, we commit ourselves to certain principles of valid argument, namely the accepted principles or laws of formal logic. Thus, for example, the fact that from 'if *p*, *q*' it follows that 'if *not-q*, *not-p*' must be explained as arising from our rules for the use of

[1] See, in particular, ch. 1, pt. I.

'if' and 'not' in English and for corresponding words in other languages.

Such a theory has obvious attractions. Common sense recoils from any purely conventionalist theory of logic, from any view that the so-called laws of logic are arbitrary or merely convenient. The theory under consideration does no obvious violence to common sense. Its adherents recognise that we do not *choose* the principles to which our arguments are to conform, if they are to be valid. At the same time, logic loses some of its mystery. Although logical laws are not of our choosing, we are given an alternative to what may be called the traditional view, that they are the most general 'laws of being' to which the universe conforms and of which we are aware by intellectual insight. On the linguistic-conventionalist theory, logic, although not itself conventional, springs from, or rests on, that which is conventional, namely the system of rules which we observe when we speak and write in natural languages. It should be noticed that the word 'rules' is here used in a justifiably extended sense. To say that there are rules of language means no more than that, in the course of time, more or less fixed meanings come to be attached to words, and more or less fixed ways of combining them to form phrases and sentences come to be adopted. When new words are invented and given precise meanings, or when we find it convenient to set precise limits to the use of an existing word, rules may be said literally to be laid down for the use of those words. But it is reasonable to apply the same word 'rules' to the restrictions which standard usage through the course of time imposes on the use of language generally.

Those who support this theory hold that logic may be divided for convenience into the formal and the non-formal, even though it is perhaps not possible to draw a clear dividing line between them. The subject-matter of formal logic will be the investigation of those general logical laws which hold in virtue of the meanings of the structural words and the syntax of natural languages, while implications that are to be explained as arising from the meanings of content- or subject-matter-words, as opposed to structural or formal words, will constitute non-formal logic.

Formal words I take to be 'all', 'some', 'if', the copula 'is', 'and', 'or', 'not'. Non-formal logical relations are limitless and do not fall within the scope of the formal logician. In Mr Strawson's words "the logician is not a lexicographer. He is not called upon to include in his books the general entailments created by every introduction of a new technical term into the language. This is a job for the specialist; the job of making clear the meanings of the words peculiar to his subject-matter. The logician's interest is wider. He is concerned with types of inconsistency, types of validity and invalidity, which are not confined to discussion of any one particular kind of subject, but may be found to occur in discussions of utterly heterogeneous topics. So the entailments of words like 'married' and 'bachelor', which carry on their face the limitation of their employment to discussions of a particular kind of subject-matter, will not, as such, figure in his lists. The sort of rules you may expect to find there are rules such that the knowledge that any one of them has been broken in a certain piece of discourse gives no clue as to what that piece of discourse is about."[1]

On this theory, then, some inferences are valid in virtue of the meanings of formal or structural words, others in virtue of the meanings of non-formal, content-words. There are thus two kinds of strict deductive inference, and attempts to reduce all inference to formal inference are misguided. The rule that 'X is a younger son' entails 'X has a brother' is not a logician's rule. But such an entailment, according to the theory, is irreducible; it cannot be represented as an exemplification of a principle of formal logic.

We may now begin to consider if this theory of the basis of logic or, to use Mr Strawson's phrase, of 'what makes logic possible', is acceptable.

'Non-formal' logic

I shall start by examining an alleged example of non-formal implication, 'If Tom is a bachelor, he is not married', and with it the view that its logical truth depends, at any rate in part, on the meaning of the word 'bachelor'. To this view we subscribe, perhaps unconsciously, whenever we make such assertions as "'Tom is a bachelor so he cannot be married' is true by definition"; and to reject the theory is to be committed to denying that any propositions whatsoever are true by definition.

[1] P. F. Strawson, *op. cit.*, pp. 40 and 41.

It will not be out of place here to recapitulate some of the conclusions which were reached in the last chapter: propositions, though expressed in sentences, are not sentences; when we say that a proposition is true, we do not mean that the stating or asserting of it is true or, again, that the words uttered are true; even though they speak different languages, Frenchmen and Englishmen can consider, accept or reject the same propositions; we can study the arguments of a foreign author in a reliable translation; it is not true of any proposition that it can be expressed only in one particular language.

Now, even if we assume that all these conclusions are true, we have no grounds for denying that, if the word 'bachelor' is used in its usual sense (and not, for example, as an abbreviation for 'Bachelor of Arts'), that Tom is a bachelor implies that he is unmarried or, to put it differently, that the sentence, "If Tom is a bachelor, he is not married", expresses, or can express, a logically necessary proposition. At the same time, the same proposition— that if Tom is a bachelor, he is not married—can, as we have seen, be expressed in other languages than English; and this at once sets (or appears to set) a problem for those who maintain the theory under discussion. How could the proposition in question be true in virtue of the meanings of all or any of the words that occur in the English sentence used to express it, if it can equally well be expressed in a sentence of another language in which none of those words occurs?

The answer might be given that the proposition, when expressed in English, is true in virtue of the meaning of the word 'bachelor' and, when expressed in French, in virtue of the meaning of the equivalent French word ('*célibataire*', perhaps). Yet if the same proposition can be expressed in different languages, it is strange that there are different reasons for its truth—as many reasons, in fact, as there are languages in which the proposition can be expressed.

This last conclusion we should reject. It seems to rest, in part, on a confusion about the use of language. The sentence, "If Tom is a bachelor, he is not married", is composed of words, but it can be used to express a proposition that is not *about* words. By contrast, the sentence, "'Bachelor' is a word that we use to designate an unmarried man", is used to express a contingent proposition about the word 'bachelor'. But it is easy to slip into the mistake of thinking that some propositions of the first sort are propositions of the second sort, and that the proposition that if Tom is a bachelor he is not married is covertly a proposition about the word 'bachelor' and is therefore true because 'bachelor' means just what it does mean. Though I think that it is altogether mistaken to draw this conclusion, it is not unintelligible that we should do so. Clearly it is the case that if I did not understand the meaning of the word 'bachelor', I should not recognise what proposition was being put forward or that it was a logically necessary one. Again, it is true that, when I hear the sentence, I may be momentarily checked before I achieve full comprehension. So it *can* be said that I understand what proposition is being asserted and see that it is logically necessary because I know the meaning of the word 'bachelor'. But to say this is not to say that the proposition asserted is logically necessary in virtue of the meaning of the word 'bachelor'. To this point I shall shortly return.

Perhaps it would be simpler to put the problem in a different way. Are we to understand that the sentence, "If Tom is a bachelor, he is not married", expresses the same proposition as the sentence, "If Tom is an unmarried man, he is not married"? If it is acknowledged that we have here two alternative ways of expressing the same logically true proposition, it must be admitted (it seems to me) that the proposition cannot be true in virtue of the meaning of a word which need not be used in a sentence expressing it. It is absurd to claim that the proposition in question, i.e. that which can be expressed as "If Tom is an unmarried man, he is not married", is true in virtue of the meaning of the word 'bachelor'; just as absurd as to say that it is true in virtue of the meaning of the word '*célibataire*'.

It appears that those who hold the view that I am criticising are in a dilemma. On the one hand, it is open to them to admit that the two sentences express the same proposition and abandon the claim that it is true in virtue of the meaning of a word that need not be used in expressing it. Alternatively they may deny that the sentences, "If Tom is an unmarried man, he is not married" and "If Tom is a bachelor, he is unmarried", are synonymous. It seems to me that the first admission would have to be resisted since it would amount to a withdrawal from the main position. But to take up the second position seems equally unacceptable. For it is only if the sentences are synonymous or, at least, if 'being an unmarried man' is *part* of the meaning of 'bachelor', that the proposition expressed in the second sentence is logically necessary. The truth, surely, is that we recognise that the sentence, "If Tom is a bachelor, he is not married", expresses a logically true proposition because 'bachelor' and 'unmarried man' are synonymous.[1]

Let us see, if we can, precisely how confusion over the meaning of the sentence is most likely to arise. Although we could use the sentence, "If Tom is a bachelor, he is not married", to express a logical truth, it is unlikely that we should use it in this way in ordinary discourse. After all, there can be few occasions when we should want to assert, for its own sake, the truism that if a man is unmarried, he is unmarried. The most natural use of the sentence would be to instruct or remind another of the standard meaning of the word 'bachelor'. Of course, such instruction would be given less ambiguously in such a sentence as "To call Tom a 'bachelor' is to say that he is not married". Yet if we did use the original sentence in this way (and what would then be expressed would be not a logical truth but a contingent proposition about linguistic usage), but if, at the same time, we were not explicitly aware that this was what we were doing, we might easily misdescribe our own assertion as a statement that it was logically necessary that if someone was a bachelor he would be unmarried. We might then go on to say "After all, that's what 'bachelor' means". And from this, it would be easy to slip into saying that what I asserted was true because of the meaning of the word 'bachelor'.

Yet the ease with which we can confuse logical and linguistic propositions is not enough to explain fully the readiness, which I think almost everybody shares, to accept the linguistic case. As a statement of ordinary life the following cannot be faulted: "I can see that it is logically necessary that if Tom is a bachelor he must be unmarried, because I know the meaning of the word 'bachelor'". To pass from this to "The proposition expressed in the sentence, "If Tom is a bachelor, he must be unmarried", is necessary in virtue of the meaning of the word 'bachelor'", seems at first sight

[1] If a sceptic asks how we *know* that the words 'bachelor' and 'unmarried man' are synonymous, the simple answer is that *we* mean the same by them. It is we who use language who decide what are to be the meanings of the words we use.

to take no step at all, but merely to replace a sentence of ordinary language by a more unambiguous version in a specialised vocabulary.

If we consider what we are in fact entitled to say, the difference between these two statements may emerge. We are entitled to say that the sentence, "If Tom is a bachelor, he is not married", expresses the proposition which it does express because the words that constitute the sentence, including of course the word 'bachelor', mean what they do mean in standard English. If the word 'bachelor', were a synonym for 'widower' or if 'married' were a synonym for 'single', the sentence, it needs no saying, would express quite a different proposition. But to say this does not explain why the proposition which is in fact expressed by these words is a logically necessary one. In fact, it is a logically necessary proposition (as we realise when we grasp the meaning of the word 'bachelor') as being a straightforward exemplification of the Law of Identity, 'If p, then p' (or 'If not-p, then not-p').

It should now be clearer why the statement of ordinary life is free from criticism. The 'because-clause' does not explain why the proposition is necessary; it explains how the speaker can *see* that it is; he can see, in fact, that, because 'bachelor' and 'unmarried man' are synonymous, the proposition is a truism. If he is a logician he will also recognise what logical law it exemplifies. To understand the meaning of common words is a necessary precondition for grasping what propositions ordinary sentences are used to assert, but the meaning of the words in no way explains why the propositions asserted are true or false, necessary or inconsistent. The sentence, "Oliver Cromwell died in 1658", expresses the contingent proposition that it does express in virtue of the fact that the words that compose the sentence mean what they do mean. But it is no more true to say that the proposition, that if Tom is a bachelor, he is not married, is logically necessary in virtue of the meaning of the word 'bachelor' than it is to say that Cromwell died in 1658, in virtue of the meaning of the word 'died'.

Formal logic

Let us now turn to the application of the theory to formal logic. Unfortunately it is not easy to state and examine the conventionalist's case about the basis of formal logic with fairness, simply because it has seldom, if ever, been argued in detail. It is more often asserted than argued, and more often assumed to be true than asserted. Provided that the conventionalist argument for the linguistic origin of 'non-formal logic' is accepted, the conventionalist may not think it necessary to formulate fresh arguments to justify an extension of the theory. However, it seems clear that two claims are made: 1. that the principles of formal logic arise from the meanings of (or rules for the use of) 'formal words' in English and their equivalents in other languages; 2. that such words are not an *essential* but a contingent ingredient in a language. It is clear that it is harder to substantiate the second claim with respect to formal than to non-formal words. Words like 'bachelor' and 'son-in-law' are manifestly introduced as a matter of convenience into language; it could very well get along without them. But it is not easy to show that the existence of words that express the function of negation and disjunction can similarly be explained. This is what *must* be shown if the thesis that we make our own language, and thereby indirectly create our own logic, is to hold.

The question which Mr Strawson poses is "What makes inconsistency possible?". But the question is ambiguous.

1. It might be interpreted as asking how it is possible for us to infringe a logical law such as the law of non-contradiction. So understood it might be answered thus: inconsistency results if we ascribe incompatible predicates to the same subject or if we assert and deny the same proposition. In the same way the answer to the question, "How can you make a mistake in adding 4 and 3 and 3 and 7?", might be "By leaving out one of the 3's". And just as this answer would not explain how it came about that the sum of 4 and 3 and 3 and 7 is 17 and not, say, 14, so we should not explain why 'p and *not-p* cannot both be true' is a law of logic by saying that we are guilty of inconsistency when we assert and deny the same proposition. On this interpretation of the question, then, we are simply asked how we can break the accepted principles of logic. So it cannot—or, at any rate, should not—be the question as interpreted in this way that Mr Strawson is raising. For he is concerned to discover, not how we can infringe accepted logical laws, but how it comes about that the so-called principle of non-contradiction is a principle of logic at all.

So the question must be interpreted in a different way: 2. How does it come about that it is a law of logic that a proposition and its negation cannot both be true? It is clear that no answer is provided to this question by the answer that we could properly give to the question on interpretation 1. Yet I am not sure that Mr Strawson always keeps these interpretations distinct. The answer that he gives to this question I shall summarise:

One of the ways in which it is possible for us to say something inconsistent (i.e., in this context, to infringe the principle of non-contradiction) is to apply incompatible predicates to the same person or thing at the same time. We call a pair of predicates incompatible if the application of both to the same person or thing at the same time results in an inconsistency. It is natural but not inevitable for a language to have incompatible predicates in it. If a given predicate-word were applicable to anything whatsoever, that word would be useless for the purposes of description. For when we say what a thing is like (and this is one of the things which we do when we apply predicates), we not only compare it with other things; we also distinguish it from other things. Somewhere, then, a boundary must be drawn limiting the applicability of a word used in describing things; and it is we who decide where the boundary is to be drawn. Thus, it is argued, it is we, the makers of language, who make predicates incompatible. But not all predicates are incompatible. 'A is red' is incompatible with 'A is blue' but compatible with 'A is round'; 'blue' and 'red', then, may be said to fall in the same incompatibility-range. So when we apply a predicate to something, we implicitly exclude from application to that thing the predicates which lie outside the boundaries of the predicate we apply, but which are in the same incompatibility-range. So we are to conclude that one way in which inconsistency can arise is for us to assert of the same subject incompatible predicates at the same time; and it is we, the makers of language, who find it convenient so to limit the application of predicates that the application of one is incompatible with the application of others. Thus, by our own unnecessitated language-making, we have created the conditions which give rise to one very general type of inconsistency.[1]

[1] P. F. Strawson, *op. cit.*, pp. 5–7.

It is difficult to avoid the conclusion that Mr Strawson is some-times considering the question "What makes inconsistency pos-sible?" on interpretation 1. and not on interpretation 2. If so, then at those times his argument is irrelevant to his purpose, if, as I assume, his purpose is to show that the laws of logic are in some sense generated by or grounded in linguistic rules. Yet this is not the only difficulty.

Inconsistency can occur, we are told, so long as the language in which we speak comprises incompatible predicates; moreover it is we, the language-makers, who decide where the boundaries limiting the applicability of predicate-words are to be drawn. But this, although true, does not show that the possibility of inconsistency arises from our language-making decisions. We decide only *where* the boundaries are to be drawn, not *that* there are boundaries to be drawn. On this point Mr Strawson is inconsistent. At first he says that it is not necessary, but very natural, that a language should have incompatible predicates in it. Yet in the same paragraph he asserts that a language *must* contain incompatible predicates: "Somewhere, then, a boundary *must* be drawn, limiting the applicability of a word used in describing things" (my italics). For, as he rightly observes, if a word were applicable to anything whatever, it would be useless for the purposes of description. Indeed if every proposition we asserted were compatible with every other proposition (as would be the case if all propositions were of subject-predicate form and all predicates were compatible), we should not be able to communicate at all. In admitting this point Mr Strawson undermines his own case.

To say that it is we who decide where the boundaries of applica-tion of predicates are to be drawn does nothing to meet this diffi-culty. It would not be surprising if an adjective in one language had no exact synonym in another language; it appears to be the case, for example, that the range of application of Latin colour-words does not exactly correspond with the range of application of colour-words in English. But inconsistency is equally possible for the speaker of Latin and for the speaker of English. What makes it possible for us to make inconsistent statements is the fact that boundaries for the application of words are and must be drawn somewhere. I can-not see that Mr Strawson has done more than draw our attention to the fact that whether the statements "John's book is orange" and

"John's book is red" are or are not inconsistent depends on the way in English we decide to use the words 'orange' and 'red'. Nothing has been said to show that the logical law, that a proposition and its negation cannot both be true, is generated by such language-decisions as these.

One thing is clear. Mr Strawson neither gives nor claims to give a fully-argued statement of the linguistic-conventionalist theory of the basis of formal logic. Thus he says that "*one* of the ways in which it is possible to say something inconsistent is by applying incompatible predicates to the same person or thing at the same time". No doubt he would be prepared to admit that there are other ways; for the account that he gives could not explain the possibility of inconsistency in propositions that are not of subject-predicate form (existential and identity propositions, for example) and therefore have no predicates, compatible or incompatible. Yet it is hard to see how any extension of the theory to allow for propositions of other forms would dispose of the objections that have been raised. I do not think that more could be shown than that we can infringe logical laws in other ways than by the application of incompatible predicates.

Even if we were to allow that our language-making decisions generated logical laws, it is at first sight surprising that Mr Strawson should have illustrated this alleged process by referring to the particular language-making decisions which determine the range of applicability of predicate-words. For, although propositions of subject-predicate form are inconsistent when their predicates are incompatible, it is even more obvious that pairs of propositions are inconsistent when one is the negation of the other. In other words, we most naturally illustrate inconsistency by citing pairs of propositions of the form 'p' and '*not-p*' rather than pairs of the form, 'x is f', 'x is g'. We may wonder, then, why illustrations of such limited application were chosen. One would have expected a logical conventionalist to explain the principle of non-contradiction by seeking to show that it arises from the rules we have laid down for the use of the word 'not' and synonymous words in other languages. One may perhaps guess why this course was not followed.

To hold that logical laws are generated by our language rules is, it seems to me, to commit oneself to the view that there could be a 'pre-logical' language in which such language rules are laid down. For the conventionalist claim is that we can get behind logic to that on which it rests. If it were a precondition for the significance of *all* utterances that the thoughts that they expressed conformed to logical laws, we should be merely wasting our time if we pretended to base those laws on language-rules, since, *ex hypothesi*, these rules to be significant would themselves have to be framed in conformity with logical laws.   Thus I assume that supporters of the conventionalist theory would maintain the possibility of a pre-logical language. But it is hard to avoid thinking of the word 'not' and the function that it performs as a *necessary* ingredient in all languages however primitive. If that is so, and if it is in terms of negation and the words that express it that the principle of non-contradiction is to be explained, then the conventionalist theory must be abandoned. For to admit that the principle *is* a logical law which holds for all thought expressed in a language in which the function of negation is expressed, and at the same time to admit that negation is not a contingent, but a necessary, function of the expression of thought is to admit that at least one logical principle does not rest on contingent rules for language.

Herein, it may be, lies the explanation of Mr Strawson's un-obvious line of argument. It seems to be held that there could be a primitive language which lacked negative terms, a 'pre-negation', pre-logical language, and that in this language incompatible propositions would be expressible and, hence, inconsistency would become possible. On such a view we should think of the word 'not' and its synonyms in developed languages as having been introduced (or as being capable of being introduced) as a breath-saving device which enables us to exclude the application to the subject of predicates incompatible with a given predicate. Thus, if I wished to express disagreement with the proposition, 'This object is red', instead of specifying the different colour of the object, I could say, "The object is not red". In this sentence, 'not-red' would serve as a substitute for 'blue' or 'yellow' or 'green' etc., and on this view negative propositions would constitute one kind of affirmative proposition. However unsatisfactory this argument may seem, it is difficult to see how else negation can be argued to be a derived and not a primitive concept. And this must be shown if the theory, so far as the principle of non-contradiction is concerned, is not to collapse. For, as we have seen, to admit both that the principle holds for all thought expressed in a language that comprises negative words, and that negation is not a contingent but a necessary function of the expression of thought is to admit that one logical principle does not rest on contingent rules for language.

In fact the argument is unacceptable. Negative propositions are not a kind of affirmative proposition. To assert that *a* is not *f*, is not to ascribe the property of '*not-f-ness*' to *a* but to deny '*f-ness*' of *a*. When we assert propositions of the form '*a* is *f*' and '*a* is not *f*', we do not ascribe two incompatible predicates; the same predicate is ascribed in one case and is excluded in the other. Of course one would not wish to deny that sentences of which predicate words have negative prefixes or suffixes can sometimes express affirmative propositions. Thus, 'nonconformist' and 'impartial' have a positive as well as a privative force, and the sentence, "The judge was impartial", can be used to express a proposition which might equally well be expressed in a sentence that lacked negative words or negative prefixes. But if we were to coin the word 'unblue', the proposition expressed by the sentence,"This box is unblue", would be affirmative and determinate only if asserted by one who had two-colour vision and saw things either as blue or as of *one* other colour. If, however, we distinguish other colours than blue, we could only use the sentence either to express a negative proposition, that the box was not blue, or to express an indefinite disjunctive proposition, 'The box is yellow or red or green or purple or . . .', where accepted rules of usage would determine the range of expansion of the disjunction.

Attempts to represent all negative propositions as affirmative fail, and with them any argument that purports to show that negation is a contingent feature of language introduced to express abbreviated substitutes for specific affirmative subject-predicate propositions. Negation cannot be explained away; it is implicit in all determinate thought whatsoever. For there is no such thing as *pure* affirmative thought. To understand what it is for an affirmative proposition to be true is in part to understand that its negation is false. To see that '*p*' is true is to see that 'not-not-*p*' is true. Affirmation and negation are complementary concepts neither of which is intelligible in isolation. The function of negation is to exclude and this function of exclusion, as Mr Strawson himself has said, is implicit in all descriptive uses of language[1] and, in fact, in all expression of thought whatsoever. So to assert that an object is red is implicitly to assert that it is not other than red. Let it be said again that, though we decide how wide the range of application of a word in a language is to be, we do not decide *that* there is to be a limit to its application. We exclude when we affirm as well as when we negate. The functions of negation and affirmation must be expressible in all language however primitive.

The possibility that the version of the conventionalist case which I have been considering has been misunderstood and therefore misrepresented makes it desirable to frame a more general criticism that is less tied to the details of that particular presentation of the theory. This is, I think, possible.

According to the version of the theory which has been considered, we are entitled to say that logical statements 'rest on' linguistic rules or that linguistic rules 'lie behind' logical statements. And although these metaphorical expressions occur in the vocabulary of a single exponent of the theory, they would, I think, be acceptable to other linguistic-conventionalists. What precisely is this relationship between language-rules and logical laws? It seems to be meant that in adopting the rules of language which we do adopt we *commit ourselves* to the acceptance of the agreed laws of logic. And I can only conclude that to say this is to say, in other words, that linguistic rules *entail* logical principles. If this conclusion is correct, the theory as a whole can be shown to be untenable.

Let R_1 stand for a particular linguistic rule and L_1 stand for a particular logical law which (it is alleged) rests on or is entailed by R_1. We can express this claim briefly as 'R_1 entails L_1'. But this is itself a logical statement and therefore it too must, according to the theory, rest on a further linguistic rule. Let us call this second rule R_2. We can now make the further claim 'R_2 entails that R_1 entails L_1'. It is clear, of course, that we have embarked on an infinite regress. If the logical proposition, 'R_1 entails L_1', rests on R_2, the logical proposition to the effect that it rests on R_2 must itself rest on a linguistic rule R_3 and so on *ad infinitum*. In order to relate a law

[1] P. F. Strawson, *op. cit.*, p. 7.

of logic to a rule of language we must always relate it in accordance with a principle of logic. If from the fact that we use language in a particular way it follows that a logical law must hold, it must follow *logically*, that is to say, in accordance with a logical law. Any attempt to base logical principles on something more ulti- mate, whether it be our system of contingent rules for the use of language or anything else, must be self-defeating. For the attempt consists of deducing conclusions from premisses and for deduction to be possible the prior validity of logical laws is a pre- requisite.[1]

We may now sum up the objections to the linguistic-conven- tionalist theory, bearing in mind the application of that theory to a particular logical law. The argument that the law of non-contra- diction rests on our rules for the use of negative expressions requires us to accept that it is possible to conceive a language in which the function of negation is not initially expressed. This language would be that in which the rules for the expression of negation would be expressed. But there could be no such language, for the function of negation is implicit in all uses of language. Thus there could be no 'pre-negation' language. Further there could be no thought in any language which did not conform to the principle of non-contra- diction. We may assert the following three propositions:

1. A minimal language (by which is meant the simplest possible language in which determinate propositions can be expressed) must be equipped to express the function of negation.

2. It could not, then, be a *contingent* fact that a given language is equipped to express that function. Therefore, that it possesses that function cannot be the result of our language-making decisions or rules.

3. All determinate propositions must conform to the principle of non-contradiction, the absoluteness of which is a precondition of determinate thought at all levels.

Thus it appears that the picture which the linguistic-conven- tionalist presents us with—of men making linguistic rules in a

[1] It has been suggested that to say that linguistic rules lie behind logical propositions is to claim that they *determine* logical propositions, not that they *entail* them. I do not understand what sort of determination other than logical determination (i.e. entailment) can be meant.

pre-logical language from which arise logical principles—is an impossible one. One cannot get behind logic or base it on anything else. All significant discourse must, to be significant, conform with logical principles. To this condition, then, the making of logical rules, which is one form of significant discourse, must also conform.

7

LOGIC AND LANGUAGE: II

In the last chapter, the theory that logic rests on linguistic rules was rejected. The discussion, it will be remembered, fell into two parts, the first of which consisted of an examination of the attempt to derive an alleged example of non-formal logic from linguistic rules, the second of an examination of the attempt to make good a parallel claim in respect of a law of formal logic. In putting forward an alternative theory of the basis of logic, I shall start by reconsidering the same formal logical law—the law of non-contradiction.

Propositional logic

The function of negation, it has been argued, is a necessary constituent of all determinate thought; and any language that is capable of expressing propositions, true or false, must be equipped to express this function of exclusion as well as that of affirmation. To affirm '*p*' is to exclude the negation of '*p*'. At the same time, all thought, to be determinate, must conform to the law of non-contradiction. For on the one hand, if we did not implicitly exclude when we affirmed, every statement that we made would be compatible with the affirmation of any other proposition whatever; while on the other hand, were it not the case that, whenever a proposition was true, its negation necessarily was false, there would be no point in making statements at all. In spite of the antithesis, 'on the one hand', 'on the other hand', it is clear that we are here making not two points but one. This is intelligible because to think in terms of affirmation-negation is to think in accordance with the principle; and this is so because the function of '*not-p*' is to represent the form of a proposition that *cannot be true* if '*p*' is true. To express the principle of non-contradiction is, then, to remind ourselves of what we do when we affirm or deny.

If the principle of non-contradiction and the correlated concept of negation are, respectively, a minimal condition and a minimal constituent of all determinate thought, it is natural that we should ask if a similar account can be given of the laws of the logic of elementary propositions generally and of the concepts, other than negation, that it involves.

In *Principia Mathematica*, as we have seen, apart from the idea of 'proposition', the ideas or concepts of negation and disjunction are treated as primitive. In other words, ' $\sim$ ' and 'v' are primitive constants. Thereafter the other constants of the system, ' $\cdot$ ', ' $\supset$ ' and ' $\equiv$ ', are introduced in formulae which are definitionally equivalent to formulae in which ' $\sim$ ' and 'v' alone are used. Are we to conclude, then, that conjunction, material implication and material equivalence are genuinely derived concepts which, without conceptual circularity, can be defined in terms of disjunction and negation?

The answer is no. While ' $\sim$ ' and 'v' *may* be selected as the undefined concepts in terms of which the rest are defined, it is also possible to start from ' $\sim$ ' and ' $\cdot$ ' or from ' $\sim$ ' and ' $\supset$ ' or even from the stroke-function ' $/$ '. And it is only considerations of economy, elegance and convenience which determine whether we start from the stroke-function or from one of the three pairs of constants. The truth is that it would be impossible to understand the function of one of the original constants without understanding the functions of each of the others. It is part of our understanding of ' p v q ' to see that for it to be true ' $\sim (\sim p \cdot \sim q)$ ' is necessarily true also. To understand ' $p \cdot q$ ' is to understand ' $\sim (\sim p$ v $q)$ '. That we can think hypothetically ('if p,q ') is a precondition for our understanding of any formula in an interpreted logical system. For to grasp the significance of, for example, the formula ' $\sim (p \cdot \sim p)$ ', is to see that it asserts that *if* 'p' *is true*, ' $\sim$ p' *must be false* and *vice versa*. To understand a rule or a formula is to understand what would be the consequence *if* the prescribed condition were satisfied. Perhaps the inter-intelligibility of the concepts of propositional logic can most clearly be seen if we consider the significance of the stroke-function. To grasp the significance of ' p/q ' presupposes an

5*

understanding on our part of the concepts of negation, disjunction, conjunction and conditionality. All this may be briefly summed up: when we restrict the number of the constants which we employ in expositions of the calculus of propositions, we effect a *notational*, not a *conceptual*, simplification; in interdefining the constants we bring to light the full significance of all of them. In other words, all the concepts involved in propositional logic are inter-intelligible.

My reason for stressing the interrelatedness of the concepts involved in propositional logic will, I think, be apparent. I am concerned to show that, just as negation is essential to all determinate thought, so equally are the other concepts of disjunction and conditionality. In effect we have already seen that conjunction is as primitive as negation when we recognise that it is a condition of significance that the joint truth of a proposition *and* its negation is an impossibility, i.e. that the law of non-contradiction holds. And just as the law of non-contradiction reveals the function of negation, so the laws of the propositional calculus bring to light the significance of the concepts which the constants symbolise. The *modus ponens*, 'if both p and if p, q, then q' reveals in part what it is to think (and, *a fortiori*, to assert) hypothetically, what, in other words, the function of 'if' is. In the same way, the first axiom of the system of *Principia Mathematica*, '$(p \lor p) \supset p$', also reveals, in part, the significance of disjunction—'if p or p is true, then necessarily p is true'. To assure ourselves of the truth of this interrelation between the concepts and the laws of propositional logic all that we need to do is consider in turn the five primitive laws of the calculus and the three operational rules, from which and in accordance with which all the other laws of propositional logic can be deduced. The conclusion appears inescapable that these laws are related to all the formal logical concepts as the law of non-contradiction is related to the concept of negation. It seems equally clear that the formal logical concepts are all equally minimal requirements for the possibility of significant thought and discourse.

The differences between this view and linguistic conventionalism should not be overlooked. According to both theories there is a close connection between certain formal elements of propositions and logical laws. But, for the conventionalist, the connection holds between formal *words* and logical laws, while in this theory it is *concepts* and not words that are connected with logical laws. Further, on the conventionalist view, languages possess words expressing negation, conjunction etc., because language-users have found it *convenient* to include them in their vocabulary for ease of communication: at the same time it is argued that the presence of these words determine that the laws of logic hold. In opposition to this it has been argued that the functions of negation, conjunction etc. *must* be expressible in any language if it is to be a medium of communication at all; and that, on this account, the presence of devices in different languages for expressing these functions does not result from contingent decisions on the part of language-users. Moreover it is not argued that, for example, negation 'lies behind' the law of non-contradiction. This view, as we have seen, is self-defeating since the prior validity of logical laws is required for the derivation of those laws. Laws of logic, it is argued, can be *derived*, if at all, only from other laws of logic. As we have earlier had occasion to notice, we cannot get *behind* logic, for the validity of logical laws is an ultimate condition for all significant thought. So when, for example, we lay down rules of language—and laying down rules is one form of significant thought—our discourse accords with the laws of logic.

Predicative logic

Let us next see if an analogous account can be given of the laws of predicative logic. We have seen that when general propositions are of subject-predicate form, certain other propositions can be seen to be logically related to them. Thus the proposition, 'There are men and all men are mortal', implies that some mortals are men, and is inconsistent with (and contradictory of) 'Some men are not mortal', which is itself compatible with (i.e. does not logically exclude the truth of) 'Some men are mortal'. So, too, 'No men are mortal' implies that no mortals are men, and is inconsistent with and contradictory of 'Some men are mortal'. These examples illustrate logical laws that belong, not to the logic of elementary propositions, but to the logic of terms. These laws hold for all propositions of the same forms as those which have been quoted. Is it not reasonable to suppose that just as the laws of propositional logic are to be correlated with the primitive concepts of negation, conjunction etc. these laws are to be similarly correlated with the predicative structure of propositions? But, if an exact parallelism is to be demonstrated, it will be necessary to show that, like the function of negation, the subject-predicate structure of some propositions (but not all, of course, since not all propositions are predicative) is primitive and irreducible. With this objective in view, we shall need to consider the subject-predicate distinction more widely.

Things and attributes

We think of the world as consisting in part of things which possess attributes or qualities—of these houses and trees and men and books, which are tall and stone-built, green and shady, dark-haired and intelligent, expensive and bound in leather. That there are these things, and that they have these or other qualities, we do not simply discover, we also in part decide. If I am asked how many things there are in my room, I cannot answer my questioner until we have agreed what is to *count* as a thing. Am I to count what lies before me as one object—a chair—or as a dozen or more pieces of wood? Only when I know what system of classification my questioner means me to adopt can I answer this question appropriately. For there is no objective number of things in my room. When we have *decided* what is to count as a thing, we can *discover* how many there are. When we make such decisions we often find it convenient to create general names and so give continuity and permanence to our classifications.

A similar account can be given of qualities. A quality is a respect in which things are like or unlike one another. So the word 'green' designates a respect in which certain things—grass, leaves, emeralds—are alike and different from other things—rubies, pillar-boxes, the setting sun. Just as we can significantly talk of the number of things only after we have decided what for us are to count as individual things, so we can ask how many qualities a thing possesses only after we have agreed in what respects it is of interest to us to compare it to other things. And since there is no fixed limit to the number of ways in which it might be of interest to compare and contrast things with one another, things do not have a finite number of attributes.

Yet, although it is we, the makers of the languages in which we speak, who decide what are to count as things, and for which of the respects in which they resemble one another we shall supply common nouns and adjectives, we do not decide that there *are* things or that there *are* attributes. Nor is this something which we discover. There was no moment in my experience when I learnt, as a piece of information, that the world was made up of things possessing attributes, nor is it true that a realisation that the world was so constituted slowly dawned on me, so that I might have said "Now I realise—the world consists of things and their qualities". It is nearer the truth to say that we *prescribe* that the world is to consist of things with attributes than that we *discover* that it is so constituted. In fact neither account is true. The situation is that so long as we have had conscious experience, we have experienced the world as ordered in this way. I think that on reflection we should agree that we cannot conceive of the world in any other way than this.

The basic distinction between the individual thing, on the one hand, and attributes, on the other, is reflected in the differing parts played in language by individuating words and phrases and by general words. We refer to the individual thing by means of proper names ('John', 'London', 'the Thames', 'moderation'—which is the proper name of an attribute), by descriptive phrases in which common nouns or noun phrases are prefixed by the definite article or demonstratives ('this', 'that'), or by personal pronouns, while we use adjectives and common nouns, which, unlike proper nouns, have general meanings, for describing, characterising, classifying and identifying individual things. Things and predicates are not related as parts to a whole; if my lawn is green, its colour is not a *component* of it nor is it a sort of skin or outer covering. So a thing is neither the sum of its qualities nor an inner core to which qualities adhere. Since, as we have seen, qualities are respects in which *things* resemble one another, qualities can only be thought of as the qualities *of* things or individuals. Similarly, it is unintelligible to speak of a thing without qualities, since for that to be possible the thing would neither be like nor unlike anything else. If I am asked what a particular thing is, I can answer only by describing or classifying it.

The claim that we think of the world as a world of things and their attributes may be re-expressed then as a claim that, in order to think about the world, we need both to individuate and to describe or classify, and, for that reason, language requires individuating words and general words (nouns, adjectives, verbs). So expressed it is perhaps more readily acceptable. But there are at least two reasons why different philosophers have rejected it. Some, for whom the 'thing-attribute' distinction can be justified only as an empirical distinction, have started from the assumption which I have already mentioned, that, if it is grounded in reality at all, the distinction must be at any rate closely analogous to that between a whole and its parts. Misled by this model of explanation, they have noticed that, if all the qualities of a thing are 'abstracted', nothing would be left at all. Thus they have reached the conclusion that the thing is after all no more than the sum of the attributes. When we recognise the inappropriateness of the analogy—when, for example, we see that if a thing has a quality, we should not wish to say that the quality was *part* of the thing—we see, too, that the notion of 'abstraction' is out of place. Since qualities are not parts they cannot be removed; and, if a thing ceased to resemble other things in a respect in which it formerly resembled them, we should not be left with the same thing lacking one of its qualities but with a different thing. Attempts to isolate things from their attributes or to isolate attributes from the individuals of which they are attributes are alike based on the confusion produced by a false analogy. Certainly it is not possible, by this line of argument, to eliminate things and leave attributes as the basic constituents of the universe.

The second attempt to dispense with the notion of 'thing' or 'individual', as primitive and underived, takes the form of denying that individuating *words* or *phrases* are indispensable for a language. It is suggested that we might in principle substitute for an individuating expression (e.g. 'John Smith') a conjunction of purely general, non-individuating phrases (e.g. 'six-footer, forty-year-old, red-haired, freckled, Oxford-graduate, bilingual' etc.) extended to the point where one and only one thing in the universe satisfied it. Yet even if this cumbersome procedure were feasible, it would not show that the notion of the individual was not primitive but derived. For we could only decide that a particular conjunction of descriptive phrases was an adequate substitute for an individuating phrase, if we already thought in terms of individuals and were satisfied that the suggested conjunction of attributes was sufficient to distinguish the individual in question.

Briefly, then, the distinction between the individual and its attributes is not an empirical distinction; that is to say, we do not discover by observation that there *are* things and attributes. Nor is the distinction merely linguistic: it is not one that we have adopted as a matter of convenience in communication. It is, rather, a *requirement* that the world should present itself to us in this form for it to be thought about. But it is not a requirement that we can decide to make or not to make. We cannot, so to speak, stand outside this way of ordering our experience. So if we were to be confronted with a language different from any which we had encountered before, we should not ask *whether* it was possible to express the distinction in it but *how* it was expressed. As we have seen in an earlier chapter, modern logical theory has moved in the direction of reducing the range of individuating expressions. But even if we were to admit the demonstrative 'this' as the only 'logically proper name', the only true individuating expression to substitute for the individual variable 'x', modern logic rightly retains the individual-predicate or thing-attribute distinction.

With this distinction of individual-attribute the logic of terms is correlated, as the logic of elementary propositions is correlated with the primitive functions of thought—negation, conjunction, disjunction and conditionality. But there are other formal ingredients of subject-predicate propositions (apart from those represented by individual-variables and predicate-variables) which are relevant to the logic of terms; namely, the notions of totality and particularity, represented in the traditional notation by 'all' and 'some'. (Indeed, some logicians appear to neglect the basic subject-predicate distinction itself when they describe the logic of subject-predicate as "the logic of 'all' and 'some'").

Again there seems to be a parallelism between the logic of propositions and the logic of terms; for just as the notions of disjunction, negation and conjunction are inter-intelligible, so too are the notions of subject-predicate, totality and particularity. To understand the function of the predicate in such a proposition as 'This shiny object is hard' (and, it is to be noticed, no words expressing totality or particularity occur in the sentence) is to recognise that *at least one thing* that is hard (particularity) is shiny, but that not necessarily *all* things that are hard are shiny. Predicate-words are general words, and for a word to be general is for it to be applicable to *all* that satisfies its definition. Thus the capacity to think in terms of subject and predicate includes the capacity to think in terms of 'all' and 'some'. The notions of totality and particularity are not to be derived from the notions of subject and predicate but neither are they logically independent of them.

It is argued, then, that the form in which the world is thought of by us is that of a world of things and attributes, of subjects and predicates, and that within the framework of this distinction all our experience is ordered. We have never *learnt* that the world is so ordered nor have we *decided* to adopt the subject-predicate form as part of a convenient system of classification. 'Operating' within this framework we are at liberty to adopt further classifications. This we do when we find close enough resemblances in things to give them common names, and we find it useful to do so. While this basic distinction is *given* from the start and is not an empirical distinction but one to which our experience must, it seems, conform, we, operating within its framework, are free to adopt or reject further classifications which we find convenient. Thus, for example, we find it convenient to mark the empirical difference between a chair and a stool by giving them different common names, although there is no logical absurdity in supposing that some people have not needed to do so and have used the same common noun to refer to either. So we can distinguish pre-empirical from empirical systems of order, and it is with those of the former kind, according to this argument, that the laws of the formal logic of terms are to be correlated.

It must be clear that this theory is incompatible with the radical empiricist's view of the way in which we acquire knowledge of the world around us. On that view our minds are initially like wax-tablets or blank sheets of paper on which marks or impressions are made in our perception of the world through the senses. So John Locke asked his readers to "suppose the mind to be, as we say, white paper, void of all characters, without any ideas". He held that the mind was a purely passive recipient of knowledge that is projected on it from outside. On the contrary view that has been argued in this chapter, and was illuminatingly, if not lucidly, put forward by Kant, the mind is differently conceived, not as entirely passive, but as like a complex receiver-mechanism (though this is not Kant's analogy), which imposes on the raw material which is fed into it a form and organisation which that raw material must take if it is to be thought about. And this view, it will be clear, is to be related to the distinction, which was discussed in an earlier chapter, between facts and propositions, on the one hand, and the basic 'given' world of events and states of affairs, on the other. There it was maintained that in order to be aware of the world we must 'propositionalise' or 'factualise' it. The form (though not the content) of facts and propositions is, it is argued, determined by the pre-empirical system of order and classification of which the subject-predicate dichotomy is a very important part.

But the formal distinction between individual and attribute is not the only element in the system of order to which the world, as thought about, conforms. Aristotle observed that the predicates which are applicable to a subject are of different basic kinds. Of these kinds of predicates, or 'categories', he compiled a list of ten, which he claimed to be exhaustive. They were the categories of substance, quality, quantity, relation, place, time, situation, state, action, being-acted-upon.

With the details of Aristotle's doctrine I shall not be concerned. There is at least one important respect in which it appears to be mistaken. If I were to say "Ceylon is an island", I should, in Aristotle's view, be predicating in the category of substance. In fact, although the phrase "is an island" is a grammatical predicate, the proposition which the sentence expresses is not of subject-predicate but of class-membership form. But the doctrine is illuminating. Aristotle draws attention to the fact that there are different irreducible kinds of things which things (in the widest sense of 'things') can be said to be, and that these differences are not either invented or empirical distinctions. If, in response to my statement, "Ceylon is an island", I were asked "What is an island?", I could say "It is a piece of land surrounded by water"; and, if I am asked what *that* is, I am eventually driven back to the answer that it is a physical *thing*. But if I am then asked, "Well, what *is* a thing?", I can give no answer. In fact I have been pushed back to an ultimate formal distinction in accordance with which I classify the items of my experience. I am driven back to the 'individual'.

Similarly, if I am asked analogous questions with reference to the statement, "Tomorrow is Tuesday"—"What is Tuesday?", "It is a day", "What is a day?", "It is a period of time", "What is time?" —I am again driven back to a point where no further direct answer can be given. For just as I have neither learnt nor decided that there are individual things, so I have never learnt nor decided that there is such a thing as time. Since one could only teach that which could be learnt, if I were to encounter a being who had no idea or concept of time, there is nothing that I could say to fill the hiatus in his understanding. I cannot justifiably assume that all men of all cultures and speaking all languages mark in their vocabularies all the empirical distinctions that I make myself, but I *must* either assume that they think within the same categories that give the form to my thoughts or recognise the impossibility of communication with them.

That the principles of non-propositional logic are correlated with all the categories of thought, as I have tried to show that the laws of subject-predicate logic are to be correlated with the categorial distinctions of thing-attribute, is a suggestion that seems to be confirmed by consideration of other logical truths than those that fall within the scope of the traditional logic of terms. The necessary truth that if A acts on B, B is acted on by A, seems to reflect a categorial distinction between active and passive and not a merely linguistic convention; that is to say, it seems that it is linguistically permissible to substitute 'B is acted on by A' for 'A acts on B' only because we cannot but think that if A acts on B, B is necessarily acted on by A. Again one may wonder if it is not a logical truth that, if A is spatially contiguous with B, B is spatially contiguous with A, and one that is related to the Aristotelian category of place. It is tempting to dismiss such examples as extra-logical or trivial. But it is worth remembering that the very obviousness of the laws of propositional logic was perhaps the chief reason for the failure of traditional logicians to recognise them. A clearer correlation between logical laws and a categorial distinction can be seen in the relation between the form of implication, 'If A is more f than B and if B is more f than C, A is more f than C', and the categories of quality and quantity. Considerations such as these point to the hypothesis that the still incompletely explored logic of relations (other than those of subject and predicate) may be profitably investigated when the primitive categories are taken as the starting-point.

The fact that philosophical theories of logic are not provable does not mean that no one theory is to be preferred to any other. We have to explain our own confidence that the logic of arguments expressed in any language is the same as the logic of the arguments that we express in our own language. This confidence is more intelligible if the laws of logic are related to the formal conditions of all thought, however expressed, than if they are related to contingent linguistic decisions reached by particular language-users. If the fact that some of our thoughts take a subject-predicate form arises not from a linguistic device that certain peoples who speak Indo-European languages have decided to adopt, but reflects a form of thought which either is necessary or cannot but be thought to be necessary, we can make some sense of the assumption that propositions and facts are the same for all men, that the propositional and predicative logic which we study is of universal and not local validity. A further consideration which seems to lend support to the theory needs to be examined at greater length.

In the first chapter of this book attention was drawn to the fact that we do not learn or forget which arguments are valid and which invalid, as we learn and forget contingent matters of fact. It is understandable that a man should say that he had forgotten the name of the wife of Charles I, but not that he should say that he had forgotten that, if all men are mortal and Socrates is a man, Socrates is mortal. No logical theorist would deny this difference between logical truths and contingent truths. But conventionalism asserts a connection between knowledge of matters of fact and logical capacity which is perhaps as implausible as the denial of that difference. For it is an implication of the theory that, if a man failed to grasp the logic of an argument, it would always be possible in principle to give him factual information that would remedy the deficiency. The thesis is that logical laws rest on rules for words and forms of expression in language. But there is nothing logically absurd about the supposition that a man might be ignorant of any such rule. At the same time it is implied that if he knew the relevant rules he would thereby apprehend the corresponding logical laws.

Thus it seems to be a corollary of conventionalism that a man might be too ignorant of linguistic facts to be completely logically competent, and that if a man failed to see the logic of an argument he could always be taught to see it by instruction in linguistic facts.

We have already seen that the attempt to base a so-called law of non-formal logic on the meaning of a particular subject-matter word misfires. To teach a man the meaning of 'bachelor' does not explain why arguments of the form, 'If x is a bachelor, x is unmarried', are valid; it merely teaches him what propositions sentences of this *verbal* form express (namely propositions of the form 'if p, then p'). No light is thrown on the fact that propositions of the form 'if p, then p' are logically true. As we have already seen, only if it is already recognised that such propositions are necessary, is instruction in the meaning of the word 'bachelor' enlightening.

Now the conventionalist might be prepared to yield ground in this point without abandoning his main position. He might agree that subject-matter words do not, after all, generate laws of non-formal logic, and he might confine himself to claiming that formal logic is generated by the meanings of formal words ('not', 'if', 'all', 'some', etc.) and formal features of speech (such as the subject-predicate distinction). It could still be argued that knowledge of the use of these elements of language is all that is necessary, and that instruction in their use would be sufficient to implant in a man a recognition of the laws of formal logic. But with the rebuttal of the parallel claim in respect of 'non-formal logic' this contention has largely lost its plausibility and even intelligibility. For, as we have seen, in establishing a connection between a logical law and the rules for an expression, whether it be a subject-matter word like 'bachelor' or even a formal word like 'not', we always *presuppose* the validity of logical laws.

The theory that has been propounded in this chapter is basically simple. It is an attempt to make sense of the conclusion to which all lines of argument appear to lead, that we cannot get behind the laws of logic to anything more primitive from which they can be derived. At the same time, since, according to the theory, the primitive concepts and categories with which formal logic is correlated constitute the initial *unlearnt* (and therefore unteachable) framework within which experience is ordered, the paradox, that by learning linguistic facts we could learn to be logical, is avoided. A schoolmaster can teach a pupil how to use Greek negatives correctly, but in so doing he presupposes, and must presuppose, that the pupil already thinks in terms of negation and affirmation. He does not attempt to teach him to do this. It is because, according to this theory, the concepts of formal logic, and the logical laws in which their function is displayed, are together unlearnt prerequisites for thought that there is no stage in experience at which we learn, or could learn, facts on which logic is based.

This categorial theory of logic provides us with a basis for clarifying the distinction between the formal and the non-formal elements in propositions. Instead of merely saying that formal elements are structural, and that their occurrence in propositions gives no indication of their subject-matter, we may say that all elements are formal which express the concepts and categorial distinctions within which all determinate thought is framed and expressed. If we could determine exhaustively the full range of categorial distinctions, we should, if the theory is sound, have pointers to the directions in which further extensions in the scope of logic may occur. We already have a rough criterion by appeal to which we can at least avoid some illegitimate extensions to logic in the field of non-predicative relations.

The logic of relations

Of the relations between the terms of a proposition, other than those of subject and predicate and class-membership, some have been singled out by logicians as being of logical interest. They consist in particular of those which are called 'symmetrical', 'asymmetrical', 'transitive' and 'intransitive'.

When the fact that a relation holds from *A* to *B* entails that it also holds from *B* to *A*, that relation is 'symmetrical'. Thus equality is a symmetrical relation, since if *A* is equal to *B*, *B* is necessarily equal to *A*. The relation of 'being smaller than' is asymmetrical; if *A* is smaller than *B*, it is not the case that *B* is smaller than *A*.

A transitive relation is one such that, if it holds from *A* to *B* and also from *B* to *C*, it also holds from *A* to *C*. Implication is clearly transitive: if '*p*' implies '*q*' and '*q*' implies '*r*', then, necessarily, '*p*' implies '*r*'. 'Being in contact with', on the other hand, is a non-transitive relation; thus, if *A* is in contact with *B* and *B* with *C*, it is not necessarily true that *A* is in contact with *C*. 'Fatherhood' is an intransitive relation; thus if *A* is father of *B* and *B* is father of *C*, it is necessarily false that *A* is the father of *C*.

Some relations, it is clear, are both transitive and symmetrical or transitive and asymmetrical or intransitive and symmetrical or intransitive and asymmetrical. Yet, when we have noticed these distinctions we may well ask what their importance is for logic and how far they may lead to the formulation of new laws. Two examples may serve to show that not all 'relational arguments' exemplify laws of the logic of relations.

Let us assume that lawyers had found it convenient to create the phrase 'murder-relation' to refer indifferently either to the relation in which a murderer stands to his victim or to that in which a victim stands to his murderer. It would not of course follow from that, that each stands in the same relation to the other. It is not the same thing to kill and be killed. So although, if we were to use the phrase, 'stands in the murder-relation to' (abbreviated to '*mr*'), in accordance with its definition, a proposition expressed in the sentence-form, "If *A mr B*, *B mr A*", would be logically true, it would not be an exemplification of a special law of relational logic. For let us assume that a man failed to recognise that such a sentence expressed a logical truth; we should enlighten him by giving him the definition of '*mr*'. He would then be able to argue in accordance with the law of *modus ponens*, that since, according to the definition of '*mr*', whenever *A mr B*, *B mr A*, and since in the given case '*A mr B*' is true, necessarily '*B mr A*' is true also. The creation of the phrase 'murder-relation' would not have increased the scope of the logic of relations.

Now contrast that argument with one that superficially resembles it: 'If Mary is taller than George and George is taller than Tom, Mary is taller than Tom'. Does this argument, too, exemplify an already recognised law of propositional or predicative logic? Again let us consider what answer we should give if someone apparently failed to recognise its necessity. Is there any factual information about meanings that would enable him to see it as an exemplification of propositional or predicative logic? A difference between the two cases is at once apparent. Whereas we *prescribe* that if *A mr B*, *B mr A*, we do not prescribe that if *A* is taller than *B* and *B* than *C*, *A* is taller than *C*. We should not *tell* our questioner that such a relation holds, we should appeal to him to *recognise* that it holds. We do not lay it down as part of the meaning of any comparative adjective ('more-*f*') that when *A* is *more-f* than *B* and *B* is *more-f* than *C*, *A* is *more-f* than *C*.

Modern logicians, in classifying relations, have not always noticed the differences which are illustrated by these two examples of inference. They have sometimes confused *words* that are used symmetrically with relations that are in themselves symmetrical. The latter only are of logical interest, for with them alone (and not with all of them), valid forms of relational inference are correlated. To blur the distinction is to open the way to indiscriminate and illegitimate extensions to the 'logic of relations' and to fall into the opposite error to that to which traditional logicians were often liable, namely the error of assuming that *all* 'relational inferences' were exemplifications of laws of subject-predicate logic. The theory of this chapter suggests a criterion for distinguishing genuine from spurious extensions to relational logic. It is to the 'relational inferences' which reveal the unlearnt categorial framework of thought that we must look to find irreducible laws of the logic of relations. Thus the fact that we think of the world in terms of the categories of quantity and quality (and of both as admitting of differences of degree) is reflected in our recognition of the *underived* logical law that whatever *A*, *B* and *C* may be, and whatever quantity or quality '*f*' may be, if *A* is *more-f* than *B*, and *B* *more-f* than *C*, *A* is necessarily *more-f* than *C*.

The classification of relations as transitive, symmetrical etc. cannot be counted as pure gain to logical theory. In the first chapter of this book it was argued that it is illuminating to say that particular arguments are valid in that their component propositions are of this or that form. Thus 'Tom is Australian' and 'Tom is not Australian' are inconsistent as being contradictions or (we may say) as being of the forms '*p*' and '*not-p*'. To isolate the forms of propositions is, in part, to *explain* the logical relations in which they stand to one another. Now it is easy to assume that transitivity and symmetry are formal properties of relations by reference to which we may explain the logical relations in which 'relational propositions' may stand to one another. In fact, this is a false assumption. To classify entailment and 'being greater than' as transitive relations is merely to draw attention to the fact that, for any terms *A*, *B* and *C*, if *A* stands in either of these relations to *B*, and *B* stands in it to *C*, then necessarily *A* stands in it to *C*. In describing entailment as transitive we have not discovered a formal property of the relation of entailment, which it shares with other relations, *in virtue of which* 'transitively relational' logical propositions hold good. As Mr Strawson rightly says, "To call a statement transitively relational in form is not to give a reason why it can play a certain role in a certain type of inference. On the contrary, we call it transitively relational just because it can play such a role; to call it transitively relational *is* to say that it can play such a role."[1] Briefly then, by the words 'transitive' and 'symmetrical', we group together diverse kinds of relations; we have not hit upon identical formal features in virtue of which transitively relational and symmetrically relational inferences are valid.

But even if we avoid the error of describing transitivity and symmetry as formal properties by reference to which the validity of arguments can be explained, we may easily fall into a different mistake. This we do if we argue in some such way as the following:

> We have seen that it is a mistake to think of transitivity as a property by reference to which the validity of a wide range of relational arguments can be explained. For all that, if transitivity is a property at all, it is surely a *formal* property, and it is reasonable to assume that what is true of transitivity is also true of all other so-called formal properties. From this we may conclude that, in Strawson's words, "Logical form is not a property which statements have *on account of which* (or in virtue of which) they have certain formal powers. Their possession of a certain form *is* their possession of those powers."

The mistake here lies 1. in assuming that transitivity is properly called a formal property, 2. in arguing from that premiss to the conclusion that there are *no* genuine formal properties by reference to which the validity of valid arguments is to be explained. I shall not repeat here my arguments on the relation between form and

[1] P. F. Strawson, *op. cit.*, p. 56.

validity. What, I hope, is clear is that, until a closer investigation of the logic of non-predicative relations has been made, the introduction into the vocabulary of logic of the classifications, 'transitive', 'symmetrical', and so on, is more likely to confuse than to enlighten the student of logical theory.

Alternative logics

It is not necessary that we should hold a categorial theory of logic to reject the notion that there might be alternative systems of logic. It is enough that we should clearly distinguish between *rules*, on the one hand, which are 'laid down', 'adopted', 'modified' and 'broken', and *principles*, on the other hand, which are recognised as binding and cannot be accepted or rejected at will. We can, of course, create fresh systems of rules (as we do when we invent a new game) or devise new logical notations, but, if the laws of logic display the conditions under which alone it is possible to think and argue significantly, the possibility of alternative logics is excluded. In fact the categorial view allows for the possibility of alternative logics. For all that the theory claims is that logic determines the formal limits of facts and propositions; that is to say, it holds for the world as it is thought about by us. Thus the logic of the syllogism holds for a world of discourse in which experience is ordered within the subject-predicate framework. If we were to say that syllogistic logic holds absolutely for all possible worlds, we should thereby deny that it was conceivable that there could be rational beings for whom experience was ordered differently. If the categorial view is sound, we cannot conceive how else experience could be ordered or what alternative system of logic there might be. But there is no logical inconsistency in conceiving that there might be other forms of order and in consequence other systems of logic. The claim to which acceptance of the theory commits us is that the logic of elementary propositions holds for all thought that takes the form of propositions, true or false, and that the logic of predication holds for all beings who think in terms of individuals and attributes.

8

LOGICAL NECESSITY

What does it mean to say that a proposition is logically necessary? To this question our discussion of logical principles has so far provided no direct answer. What is perhaps surprising is the fact that the absence of an answer to it has not, apparently, been a bar to the discussion of logical problems. Let us consider why this is so. When we say that we do not understand the meaning of a word or phrase, we normally mean, not only that we cannot define it, but also that we do not know how to use it in practice. So, if someone said that he did not know the meaning of the word 'pejorative', we should normally assume that he meant that he could neither provide a dictionary definition nor use it appropriately in conversation.

But there is a sense in which a man might be said not fully to know the meaning of a word even though he could use it correctly enough in practice. So, for example, a child might be able to identify the adverbs in a paragraph of a reading-book but fumble when asked to explain clearly what, if anything, was common to the words picked out which entitled him to call them all adverbs. If an educated person, who spoke English as his native language, said that he did not know the meaning of the word 'true' (or 'what truth is'), we should not assume that he lacked the understanding of the word 'true' that is necessary for him to carry on ordinary conversation. The ignorance, which he would be admitting to, is different from the ignorance of the man who confesses that he does not know the meaning of 'pejorative'. The former sort of ignorance, that is to say, the ignorance of the man who does not know 'what truth is', seems to be quite irrelevant to the ability to use the word correctly, since, in asking ourselves what truth is, we are not looking for some final dictionary definition by reference to which we shall always be able to use the word correctly in all circumstances. Our interest is not practical at all. When philosophers have suggested that truth is a correspondence between statements and facts or reality, they are seeking to make the concept of truth more intelligible by comparing it to other concepts, by establishing 'family relationships' between it and other concepts, or by displaying it as falling into a particular place in a hierarchy of concepts. Sometimes the investigation of a concept consists in the attempt to show that it is complex and, in some sense, definable in terms of other concepts which are accepted as primitive and unanalysable.

The question, 'What is logical necessity?', is like the question, 'What is truth?'. When we ask it, we are not primarily looking for a definition by appeal to which we can tell if a given proposition is logically necessary or not. We look for analogies between it and other notions, we ask ourselves if it is a simple or a complex notion and (if it is complex) in terms of what simpler notions it can be defined or analysed. The purpose of this enquiry is to gain comprehension for its own sake, and this we think we achieve progressively as we see how it and other concepts are interrelated. But there is also a practical reason for the investigation, and one for which there is perhaps no analogue in investigations into the notion of truth. Although we generally find no difficulty in deciding which propositions are and which are not logically necessary, this is not always so. One may confidently assert that two straight lines cannot enclose a space, but not feel confident about what *kind* of necessity (or impossibility) one is asserting. It may be possible, by examining further the notion of logical necessity, to go some way towards establishing differences between logical and other sorts of necessity.

In this chapter I shall briefly consider two topics which have sometimes been thought to throw light on the notion of logical necessity: first, the relation of logical impossibility to contradiction and self-contradiction; second, the notion of analyticity.

Logical necessity and self-contradiction

It has often been maintained that a logically necessary proposition is one the contradictory of which is self-contradictory. Further, it is sometimes argued that this statement not only makes clear what propositions are logically necessary but also what the phrase 'logically necessary' means. Thus, Mr Strawson says, "To say that a statement is necessary, then, is to say that it is the contradictory of an inconsistent statement".[1] If these contentions are acceptable our enquiry can begin and end with the arguments for them, since, if they are true, they provide us with all the answers which we need. We shall have both a definition of logical necessity and a practical criterion by which to decide if any given proposition is properly to be classified as logically necessary.

Let us see how we may come to make the statement in question. Mr Strawson notices that if we consider the different kinds of proposition that by common agreement are classified as logically necessary (e.g. 'if p then p', 'if p then not not-p', 'if no X is Y, no Y is X', 'if all M is P and all S is M, then all S is P'), we find that, different as they may be in other respects, they have one point in common, namely that in every case it would be inconsistent to assert the premiss or premisses and deny the conclusion. "To say that the steps are valid, that the conclusion follows from the premises, is simply to say that it would be inconsistent to assert the premises and deny the conclusion." "To say that one statement entails another is to say that it would be inconsistent to make the first and deny the second."[2]

Now, if we were asked to illustrate inconsistency, the sort of situation which we should most naturally cite would be one in which a proposition and its negation were both asserted, whether by different speakers or consecutively by the same speaker. In other words, the most obvious cases of inconsistency (i.e. cases of what would be logically impossible) are contradictions or self-contradictions. To contradict oneself is the most obvious and perhaps the commonest kind of logical blunder. Indeed it is so obvious that, instead of saying "It is logically impossible that so-and-so" or "It is inconsistent to say so-and-so", we often say, instead, "It is self-contradictory to say so-and-so" or "It is contradictory to say so-and-so". In other words we come to use 'logically impossible', 'inconsistent', 'self-contradictory' and 'contradictory' as roughly synonymous. But the rough synonymy of these words in ordinary

[1] P. F. Strawson, *op. cit.*, p. 22.
[2] P. F. Strawson, *op. cit.*, pp. 13 and 19.

language is misleading. They can also be used in a stricter sense and, when they are so used, 'inconsistent' (or 'logically impossible') and 'self-contradictory' (or 'contradictory') have different functions. To say, in a strict sense, that it would be inconsistent to assert *A* and deny *B* is to say that it would be logically impossible for *A* and the negation of *B* both to be true, but it would not be to say that *A* and the negation of *B* are contradictories or even contraries.[1] To say, however, that *A* and *B* are contradictories is to say that *A* is the negation of *B*. It is not difficult to show that when we use these words with precision their functions are different. We can say significantly that it is inconsistent to assert and deny the same thing. But if 'being inconsistent' *meant* 'asserting and denying the same thing' (i.e. contradicting oneself), then one would have succeeded in saying no more than that to assert and deny the same thing is to assert and deny the same thing. In fact the function of the word inconsistent (or 'logically impossible') in such a sentence is to assert the logical impossibility of asserting and denying the same thing.

It should be noticed that the words 'contradictory' and 'self-contradictory' are used in three distinguishable ways:

1. They are used to refer to pairs of propositions which exemplify the forms '*p*' and '*not-p*'.
2. They are used as terms of 'logical appraisal' (to use Mr Strawson's phrase); in such cases to say that an argument is self-contradictory or contradictory is to condemn it, to say that logically it 'will not hold water'.
3. They are used in a composite sense which combines the senses of both 1. and 2. Thus "Such-and-such an argument is self-contradictory" is often used to say that an argument is logically impossible (i.e. is self-contradictory in sense 2.) in that it involves a contradiction (i.e. is contradictory in sense 1.).

But it is very easy to blur the distinction between these three uses. When we do so we slide from the recognition that two propositions are self-contradictory in the second sense into the confused assumption that they are also contradictory in the first sense. And, as a

[1] Unless we define as contraries any pair of propositions which cannot both be true but can both be false.

result of this slide, we may be misled into thinking that all logical errors are infringements of the principle of non-contradiction.

The temptation to think that all the laws of logic are in some sense specifications of the most obvious of them, the principle of non-contradiction, is attractive most of all, perhaps, to the logical conventionalist. For, if it could be shown to be true, his task would be greatly simplified. In order to establish that formal logic rests on linguistic rules he would need only to show that this one law is generated by our rules for the words and symbols that are used in its formulation. Thereafter, the other laws of logic could be derived from it as theorems. Yet no systematic logician has ever claimed to derive all the laws of logic from the law of non-contradiction. In fact it is an impossible task. If from the premisses, 'p' and 'if p, q', I claimed to conclude '*not-q*', or from the premisses 'All M is P' and 'Some S is M' I claimed to conclude 'No S is P', I should have committed a logical blunder. But the inconsistency involved does not consist of transgressing the principle that a proposition and its contradictory cannot both be true. 'No S is P' is not the contradictory of 'All M is P and Some S is M'; it is the contradictory of 'Some S is P' which is the logical consequence of the premisses but is not identical with them. The law that has been transgressed is not the law of non-contradiction but a law of the logic of terms. I can only use the words 'contradictory' and 'self-contradictory' to condemn the invalid step, if I use them in sense 2. And since that is so, it is better that we should use a less misleading vocabulary and say, instead, that the conclusion is invalid or logically impossible.

The sentence, "A logically necessary statement is one the contradictory of which is self-contradictory", expresses either a false proposition or one that is trivial. If it is intended to express the proposition that logically necessary propositions consist solely of those the negations of which are contraventions of the law of non-contradiction, it is false. If, on the other hand, the word 'self-contradictory' is to be understood in sense 2. (i.e. as equivalent to logically false), the proposition expressed is true but trivial. It throws no light on logical necessity to say that the contradictories of logically necessary propositions are logically false any more than it throws light on truth to say that a true proposition is one the contradictory of which is false. But even if it were the case that all logical error consisted of infringements of the law of contradiction, so that it would be true that only self-contradictory propositions were inconsistent, we should not have discovered the meaning of 'inconsistent'. If we were to discover that only things that had the property *f* also had the property *g*, we should, to use a traditional distinction, have discovered the *extension* of '*g*-things', not the *intension* of *g*; more simply, we should have discovered what things *were g*, not what it means to say a thing has the property *g*. To say that only pleasant things are worth pursuing is not to say that 'pleasant' *means* 'worth pursuing'. The general conclusion to be drawn is that the alleged definition which we have considered throws no light on the meaning of 'logical necessity'.

Analyticity and logical necessity

Let us turn next to consider the application of the word 'analytic' to logically necessary propositions. The classification of propositions as either analytic or synthetic is due to Kant. He said, in the *Critique of Pure Reason*, "In all judgments in which there is a relation between subject and predicate that relation can be of two kinds. Either the predicate B belongs to the subject A as something contained (though covertly) in the concept of A; or B lies outside the sphere of the concept of A, though somehow connected with it. In the former case I call the judgment analytic, in the latter synthetic. Analytic judgments (affirmative) are therefore those in which the connection of the predicate with the subject is conceived through identity, while others in which that connection is conceived without identity, may be called synthetic."[1] As an example of an analytic judgment, Kant quotes 'All bodies are extended' and, as an example of a synthetic judgment, 'All bodies are heavy'.

We do not need to examine Kant's account in detail. The language in which he expresses the distinction is vague and in part metaphorical. It is, for example, not easy to state precisely what he meant when he said that one concept was contained covertly in another concept or that a concept might be 'outside the sphere' of another concept. But, even if there are obscurities in his view, it is possible to be clear about his general position. The distinction he draws is not that between necessary and contingent propositions.

[1] *Introduction*, section IV.

Although analytic propositions are necessary, so too, in Kant's view, can certain synthetic propositions be necessary. Thus, even although the concept of 'having a cause' is not, in Kant's view, covertly contained in the concept of 'event', the proposition, 'Every event has a cause', is for Kant necessary (or *a priori*). Thus he insists on the possibility of synthetic *a priori* propositions as well as analytic *a priori* propositions. So to say that a proposition is analytic is not to say *that* it is necessary but, in some sense, *why* it is necessary. The criterion for analyticity that he provides is two-fold: first, the predicate-concept must be covertly contained in the subject-concept; second (and perhaps in consequence), analytic propositions are of such a kind that to deny them would be to involve oneself in self-contradiction. For this is presumably his meaning when he says that the connection of the predicate with the subject is conceived through identity. It is clear that Kant considered that 'All bodies are extended' satisfied both these criteria, that the predicate-concept 'extended' is covertly contained in the subject-concept 'body', and that the proposition could only be denied in contravention of the law of non-contradiction. Whether Kant would have demanded that both criteria should always be satisfied is not equally clear. Certainly if he would have accepted 'All extended substances are extended' as an analytic proposition, he ought to have abandoned the claim that the predicate-concept is contained *covertly* in the subject-concept. For the purposes of our present enquiry we do not need to reach a decision on this point.

Since he accepted the Aristotelian classification of propositions, Kant restricted the application of the words 'analytic' and 'synthetic' to propositions of subject-predicate form. It is not surprising that later modification or abandonment of the Aristotelian analysis has led to an extension of the use of 'analytic' to other sorts of proposition. But, although the word 'analytic' has become part of the standard vocabulary of logic, logicians have not agreed on a precise definition. But a sample of definitions that have been given reveals wide agreement.[1]

Thus M. Schlick says "A judgment is analytic if the ground for its truth lies solely in the definitions of the terms which occur in

[1] These definitions are quoted by F. Waismann in the first (Dec. 1949) of an important series of articles entitled 'Analytic-Synthetic', published in *Analysis*.

it".[1] A. J. Ayer says "that a proposition is analytic when its validity depends solely on the definitions of the symbols it contains";[2] A. C. Ewing, more briefly, says that an analytic judgment is one which follows from the definition of its subject-term;[3] while A. Pap says that analytic statements may be roughly characterised as statements whose truth follows from the very meaning of their terms.[4] All these definitions, taken out of context, appear to be compatible with Kant's account, if we interpret Kant's statements about subject- and predicate-concepts as being equivalent in meaning to statements about the meanings or definitions of subject- and predicate-words.

But great differences of opinion emerge when we examine the views that the philosophers who have provided these definitions hold on the relationship between analyticity and logical necessity. Kant drew two distinctions, that between analytic and non-analytic (i.e. synthetic) judgments and that between necessary and contingent judgments. In the writings of some of the philosophers who have been quoted these two distinctions tend to be telescoped into one. It is assumed that only analytic propositions are necessary and that all non-analytic propositions are contingent. Thus the continuation of the sentence in which Ayer defines 'analytic' was "and synthetic when its validity is determined by the facts of experience". At the same time the difference in meaning between 'analytic' and 'necessary' has not entirely disappeared. For when Ayer says that the truths of logic and mathematics are analytic propositions, he is clearly not intending to present us with the truism that analytic propositions are analytic or that the truths of logic are truths of logic. On one interpretation of his argument, the notion of 'necessary truths' remains uninterpreted. But the distinction disappears entirely in the writings of philosophers for whom not only 'analytic propositions' and 'logically necessary propositions' are co-extensive, but also the words 'analytic' and 'logically necessary' are synonyms. This stage is reached by Strawson when he says "Variants on 'logically necessary statement' are 'analytic statement',

[1] M. Schlick, *Allgemeine Erkenntnislehre*, 1st ed., 1918, p. 97.

[2] A. J. Ayer, *Language, Truth and Logic*, 2nd ed., 1950, p. 78.

[3] A. C. Ewing, *Short Commentary on Kant's Critique of Pure Reason*, 1938, p. 19.

[4] *Mind*, 1946.

6+

'necessary truth', 'logically true statement' ".[1] To accept this equation is to accept that 'necessary' *means* 'logically necessary' and that both *mean* 'analytic'.[2]

If we find this last view acceptable, we thereby take the first step towards answering the question with which this chapter opened. This step consists in asserting that 'logically necessary' means 'analytic'. We shall have answered the question entirely if we can show that it is possible to define 'analytic' without recourse to the notion of logical necessity. However, this appears to be impossible. If we say that analytic propositions are those the truth of which is guaranteed by (or follows from) the definition (or the meaning) of the words (or symbols) it contains (or in which it is expressed), we provide a definition for the understanding of which it is necessary that we already understand the notion of necessity. For to say that A 'follows from' B is to say that if B is true, then, as a matter of logical necessity, A must be true also. It would seem that all definitions of 'analytic' require a vocabulary which already comprises words expressing necessity.

Yet the principal objection to any attempt to elucidate the notion of 'logical necessity' by reference to analyticity is that there are in fact no propositions whatever that are, in the sense defined, analytic. In an earlier chapter I set out what was intended as a refutation of the theory that logical propositions rest on rules for the use of words. Now it is true that not all the philosophers who accept one or other of the definitions quoted would subscribe to a conventionalist theory of logic. But the assumption that there is a class of propositions that can be true by definition rests on the same confusion between sentences and propositions which is, or appears to be, basic to logical conventionalism. I shall not repeat at length the arguments that have already been given but confine myself to considering a particular example.

Let us consider the claim that 'All bodies are extended' is

1 P. F. Strawson, *op. cit.*, p. 21.

2 Of course this sentence can be interpreted as providing, not a statement of fact about how laymen and logicians use these ingredients of our logical vocabulary, but as expressing the author's *decision* to use the words in a particular (perhaps quite novel) way. If the sentence is used in the latter way it cannot be faulted. But I do not think that this is Strawson's intention, which I take to be to throw light on the interdefinability of words in common philosophical use.

analytic, as 'analytic' is defined by Pap, or, what comes to the same thing, 'All bodies are extended' is true by definition. If, in putting forward this proposition we mean by the phrase, 'All bodies', all substances one of the properties of which is extension, then the proposition which we assert can be expressed as "All extended substances are extended" or as "All bodies are extended", or in an indefinitely large number of other ways in different languages. The one proposition expressed exemplifies the formal law that if anything has the property f it has the property f, which can itself be regarded as a specification of the law of identity, 'for all p, if p, then p'. What makes the proposition 'All bodies are extended' necessarily true is not the fact that 'body' means 'extended substance'. The case is different. What makes the *sentence* "All bodies are extended" express the proposition which it does express (i.e. the logically true proposition that substances which have the property of extension, have the property of extension) is the fact that the word 'body' means 'extended substance'. It is not the case that the proposition in question is true because of the meaning and definition of 'body' ('by definition') but that the sentence used expresses the proposition in question because of the meaning or definition of 'body'. A little reflection will reveal that every alleged instance of 'truths by definition' is to be explained (or explained away) in the same way.

A less objectionable account of analyticity than those which have been considered is given by Waismann. "A statement is analytic", he says, "if it can by means of mere definitions be turned into a truth of logic".[1] It is a virtue of this characterisation that it makes no claim to explain the nature of logical necessity by reference to analyticity. But it cannot be considered satisfactory. To say that an analytic statement can be *turned into* a logical truth is to admit by implication that it itself is not a logical truth or that, if it is, it is at least a different logical truth from that to which it can be converted. Yet Waismann, I feel sure, would have wished to say that the proposition, 'All planets move round the sun', is itself logically true. At least he would have agreed that the sentence, "All planets move round the sun", expresses a logical truth when the speaker means by 'planet' 'heavenly body that moves round the

[1] F. Waismann, *op. cit.*

sun'; and it is only when the word 'planet' is so used that the proposition expressed would be called analytic. The truth is rather that, if it is proper to use the word 'analytic' at all to classify statements, the 'analytic statement', 'All planets move round the sun', *is* a logical truth. It is the *same* statement as that which can equally well be expressed as 'All heavenly bodies that move round the sun move round the sun', it does not need to be *turned into* that statement. It itself, and not some different statement into which it can be turned, is a logical truth.

Is there any place left in the vocabulary of logic for such an expression as 'analytic statement'? In banning it we seem to lose little except a source of possible confusion. If so-called 'analytic statements' are simply the truths of logic, and if 'truth by definition' is a phrase that has no application, would it not be best to expel it from philosophy, as 'phlogiston' was expelled from the vocabulary of natural science? Yet it has so firm a place in the language of philosophy that it can hardly be eradicated altogether.

And perhaps there is, after all, an acceptable use for the word 'analytic'. It is not quite the same thing to say "All bachelors are unmarried" as to say "All unmarried men are unmarried", even when it is intended that each sentence should be understood as expressing a logical truth. We grasp the meaning of the second sentence more readily than we grasp the meaning of the first. It was perhaps the importance of this difference that Kant had in mind when he said that the predicate-concept was *covertly* contained in the subject-concept.

The difference between these sentences is one that we might mark by characterising the first as 'analytic'. If we were to follow this course, then we should apply the word 'analytic' not to propositions but only to sentences; namely, to those sentences which, though they expressed logical truths, might seem at first hearing to express factual empirical propositions. But that a proposition was expressed 'analytically' would be not of logical but only of psychological interest.

Consideration of the relation between self-contradiction and logical necessity and of so-called analytical propositions has brought us no nearer to an answer to the question with which we began. We have not succeeded in discovering concepts which are more basic than that of logical necessity and in terms of which logical necessity can be defined. My conclusions are negative and the notion of necessity is left unexplained. There is no great difficulty in illustrating necessity by multiplying examples of relations that, we say, *must* hold; but, without claiming that the notion of necessity is genuinely primitive and can be intuitively grasped but not explained, I can see no way of reducing it to simpler terms. All that seems possible is to suggest, very tentatively, a criterion for distinguishing logical necessity from necessity of other kinds. That necessity is not exclusively a logical notion seems likely. Even if it never *is* necessary that physical changes or processes occur in this or that way, it seems hard to deny that a man might significantly ask himself, "Is it *necessary* that such-and-such substances should react in the way in which we observe them to react?". And when he asks himself such a question, he is not, it would appear, asking if a relationship were *logically* necessary. As was said earlier, one may recognise the necessity of a truth of Euclidean geometry without any clear notion of what *sort* of necessity geometrical necessity is.

In an earlier chapter a two-fold theory of the notion of logical laws was put forward. The logic of elementary propositions, it was argued, consists of the presentation of the limits within which alone it would be possible, for a being that is capable of entertaining propositions as true or false, to think significantly. It was further argued that the laws of the logic of terms are correlated with, and in a sense reveal, the primitive, unlearned and incommunicable ways or categories in terms of which we find that we think of the world. Thus it was held that the logic of subject-predicate reveals a primitive thing-attribute way in accordance with which our conscious experience of the world is ordered. These categorial principles of order were distinguished from the empirical classifications which we find it *convenient* to adopt. These latter classifications we may change and modify; they neither give rise to nor are correlated with any special logical principles.

This theory of logic suggests a possible criterion for distinguishing logical from other kinds of necessity. The suggestion is that those necessary truths are logically necessary which are to be related to the categories to which our experience conforms and to the primitive concepts of negation, conjunction, disjunction and conditionality.

The suggestion that, in order to decide if a given instance of necessity is logical or not, we should ask ourselves if it corresponds to a primitive category of thought is perhaps too imprecise to serve as a clear guide. It might, moreover, lead to paradoxical extensions of the scope of logical necessity. Thus, if we held that we cannot but think of the constituents of the physical world as being necessarily causally interrelated but, at the same time, concluded that it was our way of looking at the world that determined us to see it in that way, then, in accordance with the suggested criterion, we should have to conclude that 'every event (necessarily) has a cause' or 'necessarily nothing comes into being out of nothing' were logical truths. In the end we might be driven to the conclusion that, after all, all necessity is logical necessity and so reverse our first, common-sense assumption.

It should be noticed, however, that this conclusion would be different from that which is reached by most of the philosophers who have argued that all necessity is logical. When it is maintained that, if such a proposition as 'Every event has a cause' is necessary at all, it is logically necessary or tautologous, what is usually, if not always, meant is that it can be shown to exemplify an *accepted* logical principle (e.g. the law of non-contradiction). The conclusion to which the present line of argument points is different; namely, that the proposition exemplifies a primitive and irreducible law which is not derivable from the laws of logic as commonly accepted. In reaching such a conclusion, then, we should claim to be discovering new logical laws, not extending the applications of the old accepted laws of logic.

9

GENERALISATIONS AND THEORIES

When we have examined the forms of argument in which premisses entail conclusions and those kinds of propositions which are logically necessary, have we exhausted the scope of logic? On the face of it, there is good reason to suspect that we have not. Valid arguments do not prove the truth of their own universal premisses. The proposition, 'If all men are mortal and all Greeks are men, all Greeks are mortal', does not, of course, prove that all men are in fact mortal. But few of us are so sceptical as to deny that we can be said, for all practical purposes, to know that they are. So, if there is a class of non-necessary universal propositions which, as rational men, we are prepared to accept, it is reasonable to assume that there is some form of reasoning, not necessarily deductive, by which we can justifiably arrive at them. Even if generalising is only a convenience, and not an absolute requirement, of our day-to-day lives, the very purpose of science seems to be to establish such propositions. It would be paradoxical to the point of absurdity to dismiss all such generalisations as unjustified simply on the grounds that their truth could not be proved by deductive methods. We have the strongest incentive to accept the possibility of a kind of inference called *induction*, whereby we may legitimately pass from the recognition of the truth of a number of non-necessary propositions to the formulation of propositions of unrestricted generality or to other particular propositions. And I shall first consider the claims of this alleged kind of reasoning—induction by simple (i.e. incomplete) enumeration—to provide the guarantee that we need for asserting universal propositions, for justifiably moving in our arguments from 'Some S is P' to 'All S is P'.

No logician would try to justify all the moves from 'some' to 'all' that we may be tempted to make in ordinary life. We should distinguish propositions of restricted generality from those that are genuinely universal; propositions which are about finite, countable collections of individuals, from those, such as 'All men are mortal', which are not. That all the kites native to the British Isles nest in a single area in central Wales is a proposition of the first type. It is one that we should be justified in asserting without reservation only on the basis of a *complete* enumeration of all the individual kites born in the British Isles. And where the enumeration is incomplete we must content ourselves with a 'generalisation' in the commonest sense of that word, i.e. a proposition to the effect that something is true 'in general' or 'for the most part'. Restricted general propositions and generalisations raise no logical problems. In asserting neither can we claim to be justified if we go beyond the observed facts. The logician is not required to justify the assertion of a man who, after encountering half a dozen excitable Italians, says that all Italians are excitable, or who, when he is entitled to say 'hardly ever in my experience', says 'never'. But propositions about restricted classes, the members of which can be counted, are to be contrasted with those in which what is predicated is to be thought of as applying to whatever falls within the subject-class, whether observed or unobserved. To assert that man is mortal is to assert that whatever satisfies the condition of being a man must die. Such a proposition cannot be established by counting heads, since complete enumeration of an unlimited class is impossible, and the fact that men have died cannot entail that men *must* die. It is to explain the acceptability of such propositions as these that we are tempted to appeal to the reasonableness of induction by simple, as opposed to complete, enumeration.

Arguments incompletely expressed

The distinction between deductive and inductive arguments is not always a clear one, since in conversation we do not formulate our arguments with the rigour and completeness that is displayed in examples in logical text-books. Even when we present arguments of strict validity, it is the exception rather than the rule to express fully in words the premisses from which we argue and the conclusions which we draw. Thus, "Men are mortal and he is a man, so he must die some time" is abbreviated to "After all he's a man, so he must die some time". It would, in fact, be very wearisome if the rules of conversation demanded that we should put into words all the steps in every argument, however acceptable and familiar they were to all the parties in a discussion. So, if we are to understand the logical structure of the arguments of ordinary life, it is necessary that we should recognise that men put into words only what needs expressing or emphasising. But a too literal interpretation of what people actually say may sometimes mislead us either into suspecting logical fallacies where they do not occur, or into misclassifying deductive arguments as inductive.

To say "It will please your mother very much if you visit her when you are in London, so you ought to go" is not necessarily to commit a logical fallacy; nor is it to reason in a non-deductive way. Certainly, that a course of action gives pleasure does not *entail* that one ought to follow it; but the reasonable interpretation of such a statement is that it is a *valid* argument, the major premiss of which ('You ought to do what gives pleasure to your mother') was considered by the speaker to be too obvious to be worth putting into words. Similarly, I can say "It's foggy today, so the trains will be delayed", and be arguing not inductively but deductively from premisses one of which (that fog reduces visibility and slows traffic down) is sufficiently familiar to be left unspoken.

Yet it is sometimes thought that such sentences always express complete inductive arguments, the sort of arguments by which we arrive at the general propositions that the syllogistic analysis which I have given requires. For, it can be asked, how else can we formulate such general propositions as that fog causes delays on the railway than on the strength of such individual arguments as "It's foggy today, so the train will be late"? But the objection is unconvincing. We do not arrive at the general proposition by observing "It's foggy, *so* the train will be late" until we have satisfied ourselves of a more than coincidental connection between the incidence of fog and trains running late. We should only say, "It was foggy on such-and-such a day, *and* the trains were late". When we have satisfied ourselves that there is a causal connection, but not till then, the words 'so' or 'therefore' become appropriate. The only likely candidates

6*

for the title of 'inductive argument' that we can find here are those of the form, 'On occasion 1. it was foggy and the trains were late, on occasion 2. it was foggy and trains were late, on occasion 3. etc.; therefore *whenever* it is foggy, trains are, or will be, late'.

It is the question of the validity or invalidity (or acceptability or unacceptability) of arguments of this form that we must consider.

Induction by simple enumeration

Under what conditions, if any, is it justifiable to draw a conclusion of unrestricted generality on the evidence of particular observations? Are we, to take the most familiar example, justified in concluding, from the fact that the sun has risen once in every period of twenty-four hours throughout all the periods of time of which we have knowledge, either that it will always rise or that it will rise tomorrow? On first thought it would seem perverse to deny either that we have good grounds for making such assertions or that those grounds consist of the known instances of the sun's rising in the past. Yet, paradoxically, the mere occurrence of what can be called 'favourable instances' (i.e. those compatible with the truth of a general proposition and therefore 'favourable' to it) seems to constitute in itself no grounds for accepting a general proposition at all, as we may see if we consider an imaginary situation.

Assume that we discovered that the first client to do business at one branch-office of a particular bank on a given day was born on a Tuesday. (It does not concern us to consider how this fact could be discovered or why anyone should take the trouble to establish it.) Assume, too, that one carried one's researches further and established that the first clients at twenty-five other branches of the same bank on the same day were also born on Tuesdays, though not necessarily the same Tuesday as that on which the first client to be investigated had been born. Let us suppose, moreover, that apart from this one point of resemblance no pattern of resemblance in the life-histories of these different people emerged from our investigations. Would it be reasonable to conclude that the first clients at other branches of the same bank, not hitherto investigated, were also born on Tuesdays? The answer is, of course, no. We should assume that it was a mere coincidence that the life-histories of the clients who had been investigated shared this trivial feature.

Let us consider what we mean by describing events as 'coincidental'. We use the word when events have some feature in common for which no single common explanation can be found. Even when no single explanation can be given for all the events in question, we should not use the word if we knew (or were in a position to calculate) how it came about that each of the events possessed the common feature. Thus if Jones and Brown happened to meet without pre-arrangement in the same railway carriage, we should not describe the presence of them both as coincidental, if we knew why each might reasonably be expected to be there, even though the reasons for which each was there were different. So we tend to describe as coincidental only those events which also could not easily have been predicted. We should not have predicted that the bank's clients would all have been born on Tuesdays, and we can think of no plausible reason why they should all have been born on that one day of the week.

The conclusion to be accepted is that so long as the repeated occurrence of similar events is, or appears to us to be, coincidental, it gives us no ground for predicting or extrapolating beyond the range of our observations at all. But to accept this is to admit the truth of the paradox that the mere occurrence of favourable instances provides us with no good reason for formulating or accepting a corresponding general proposition.   Once we describe recurrences of similar events as coincidental, we reject them as evidence on which to base predictions or as grounds for general propositions.

Let us reconsider the traditional problem of explaining our confidence that the sun will rise tomorrow. We may believe that the reason why we are confident is the fact that the sun has invariably risen in the past. Yet this, I suggest, is not the true reason. In the first place we, probably unconsciously, rule out the possibility that the regularity in the relative movements of the sun and the earth in the past has been coincidental. We assume, perhaps without realizing that we are assuming, that the regularities that we have observed are the symptoms of an ordered system and not inexplicable, 'chance' occurrences in a chaotic universe. The past regularities which we have observed are not the evidence on which our rational predictions rest. The case is, rather, that we interpret these regularities as the manifestations of an ordered, intelligible system.

It is either our understanding of that system or our confidence that the observed regularities are integral to such a system (even although we may have no clear idea of what that system is), which gives rise to a reasonable belief that the regularities will continue.

Perhaps a further example will make this view clearer. In the past I have noticed that every weekday shortly after noon a fairly heavy stream of cyclists passes southwards in front of my college in Oxford. What grounds have I, or anyone else, for predicting a similar stream of traffic at the same time in the future? The answer to this question we may reach indirectly. In a situation like this it seems to be natural to us to guess or assume that the regularities which we observe are not coincidental. I assume that there is *some reason* for the traffic regularly being heavier at some times rather than at others. And this can lead me to ask what that reason is. Then it may strike me that the cyclists are coming from their work and that noon is a common time for a break for a meal. So one begins to formulate a possible hypothesis that will make it intelligible why there *should* be a stream of cyclists at that particular time of day. The confidence that I can safely predict the recurrence of similar streams of traffic grows progressively with my belief in the explanatory theory that forms in my mind. This belief is strengthened if I can see that it is compatible with facts which I already know— e.g. that there are industries which employ a great deal of labour in the direction from which the cyclists are coming, and that many industrial workers live in the direction towards which the cyclists are going.

Sometimes, of course, our understanding of a situation is too slight for us to formulate any clear-cut theory to explain a given phenomenon that repeatedly occurs. In such cases we may, after reflection, come to the conclusion that the repetitions are indeed coincidental and, in that case, we make no inferences at all. Alternatively, we may guess that there is a principle in accordance with which the repeated phenomena occur and make guarded predictions on the assumption that that belief is correct. In such a situation as that in which a series of clients of a given bank were born on Tuesdays, we should follow the first course, and it is not difficult to imagine situations in which the second course would seem more reasonable. It would be naturally followed by a man aware of the regularity of the sun's rising in the past, if he lacked all knowledge of physics and astronomy.

The reason, then, for our rational confidence that the sun will rise tomorrow is not the fact that it has risen in the past, but our belief that what we have repeatedly observed are manifestations of the workings of natural laws. To assert the general proposition that future S's will be P, or that all S's are P, simply on the grounds that a finite number (however large) of S's has been observed to be P, is to take an irrational and indefensible step. If to perform an induction is to do just this, then induction is a procedure that cannot recommend itself to rational human beings and therefore does not need to be justified. Yet it has often been maintained that induction *so defined* is the only rational procedure for arriving at general propositions about the world and the one by which all advances in science are achieved.

How is it that a procedure which is patently irrational has been often defended? In part the explanation lies in the fact that philosophers have sometimes failed to distinguish between rational belief and non-rational expectation, or have misunderstood the nature and purpose of scientific investigation.

Rational beliefs and conditioned expectations

Both animals and human beings can be drilled to respond in predictable ways by being repeatedly subjected to the same stimulus. If fowls are regularly fed at the same time of day, they come to expect their food at that time. By an intelligible extension of the word 'believe', they may be said to believe, when the appropriate hour of day approaches, that they will be fed. All that seems to be needed to produce such states of expectancy is the constant repetition of a pattern of events. Thus the regularity with which day follows night and night day produces in us what can be called a behavioural expectancy that the pattern will continue. This expectancy must be clearly distinguished from what I have called rational belief. Hitherto I have tried to explain what grounds we have for believing that the sun will continue to rise in the future as it has risen in the past. But it would make no sense to speak of grounds or reasons for the acquisition by animals or human beings of conditioned expectations and dispositions to behave in specific ways. Repeated similar experiences produce or cause expectations; they do not constitute good reasons for believing that such expectations are justified. Yet it would not be surprising if the causes of conditioned expectations were confused with the reasons for holding a rational belief. It is perhaps this confusion that in part explains the tenacity with which philosophers and laymen have clung to the view that the mere fact that similar events have regularly occurred constitutes good grounds for maintaining that they will continue to recur.

Scientific explanation

It is presumptuous for a non-scientist to generalise about science but, since the methods of science are said to be inductive, consideration of its nature and aims cannot easily be avoided. The aim of the scientist is to make the universe intelligible, and his success is marked by the extent to which he displays what is, or can be, observed as exemplifying the operation of interrelated laws or principles, constituting a single interrelated system. There is a close analogy between the ideal of science and the ideal of philosophy. Both are concerned to provide systematic explanations of the whole field of experience; but the scientist works within self-imposed limits which do not apply to philosophical explanations. For he regards as acceptable only those laws or suggestions for laws (hypotheses or theories) which can be empirically tested. Yet for a scientific hypothesis to be empirically testable is not for it to be completely verifiable. Complete verification of a scientific theory would indeed be impossible for two reasons.

A scientific hypothesis about, say, the properties of common salt must be understood to apply, not simply to samples of salt that have been examined, but to anything at any time that may satisfy the defining conditions of common salt. One could only completely verify a theory about a substance if there were a determinate limited quantity of it that could be inspected. Given time, I could establish completely that all the common salt in my kitchen dissolves in water, but not that whatever satisfied the definition of common salt would be soluble in water.

The second reason for not demanding complete verifiability of scientific hypotheses is, in fact, part of the first. However reluctant a scientist may be to commit himself to asserting a theory categorically, e.g. that a given substance has a particular property, what he supposes (or hypothesises) is that the substance essentially possesses the given property; in other words, that, if anything is an instance of it, it *necessarily* has that property. At best we could completely verify the statement that a finite number of *x*'s were *f*, never that all *x*'s *must* be *f*. What is demanded of scientific hypotheses is that they should, in principle, be empirically falsifiable. By this demand it is not intended, of course, that it must be possible to prove every scientific theory false, but that every such theory must be so framed that, if it is false, it must be possible to show it to be false by empirical tests.

Many philosophers since J. S. Mill have represented the principal task of scientists as that of framing generalisations, and their aim as that of describing rather than explaining the universe. Scientific laws are rightly distinguished as laws in a different sense of the word 'law' from the laws of the land which we are called on to obey; and the distinction has been marked, memorably but misleadingly, by calling laws of the former kind *descriptive* and those of the latter *prescriptive*.

It is true that the laws which science seeks to discover do not prescribe the way in which the universe is to operate, and that the movement of bodies do not *obey* or *conform to* the laws of physics. But to call those laws descriptive suggests that they are generalisations that report the ways in which bodies can be observed to behave. One motive for representing the general propositions of science as descriptive rather than explanatory is clear. Hume, the most consistent and perhaps the most influential of British empiricists, noticed the fact that, in a strict sense of the word 'see', we cannot see that one body causally interacts with another as, for example, we can see that one body is contiguous with or larger than another body. The impact of Hume's discovery on some philosophical accounts of scientific method may briefly be expressed thus: since the notion of causal efficacy is not an empirical notion it can have no place in empirical science. Thus, expressions which convey, or seem to convey, this notion should either be eliminated from scientific discourse or reinterpreted as merely descriptive. In conformity with this programme the laws and hypotheses of science were interpreted not as causally explanatory but, as we have seen, as purely descriptive generalisations.

At the same time, some philosophers have wished to have the best of both worlds and to claim that laws, being descriptive generalisations, are at the same time explanatory. But this is to claim too much. Just as the fact that the sun has risen in the past in itself constitutes no good reason for asserting that it *will* rise in the future, so it in no way explains why the sun *should* rise. If, in answer to the protest, "Why should I take my shoes off when I go into this temple?", I said "Oh, people always do take their shoes off in Buddhist temples", I might silence the questioner and dissipate his wish for an explanation. Indeed many of our apparent requests for explanations are made in the belief that the circumstance about which we are enquiring is in some way unusual or irregular, and these requests we are prepared to withdraw when it is made clear to us that it is not. But such generalisations, though they may dispose of questions, do not answer them. It is a striking characteristic of great scientists of the past that they have found problems less in the unusual than in the usual. They have been provoked to look for explanations of *ordinary* phenomena which raise no problems for ordinary life.

Many of the laws and hypotheses of science are very different from empirical generalisations. It is a generalisation that apples fall to the ground when they are ripe, and the world did not need to wait for Newton to propound it. Newton's achievement was not to assert the generalisation but to explain it. The Law of Gravitation, that every particle of matter attracts every other particle with a force proportional to the product of the masses and inversely proportional to the square of the distance between them, is not a pretentious restatement of a fact of common experience but a principle suggested by a genius according to which the observable movements of all bodies, of the planets and the sun, of the ebb and flow of the tides, can be shown to exemplify the working of a single universal law, capable of expression in a simple mathematical formula. Not all the conclusions of scientific investigation are so obviously explanatory hypotheses as the Law of Gravitation, and some seem rather to resemble the 'pre-scientific generalisations' (to use Russell's phrase) that we repeat unreflectively every day—'Apples are good for you', 'Celluloid is inflammable', 'Toadstools are poisonous'. I shall assume that science comprises laws of both these loosely-defined kinds and consider, in relation to each, what answers can be given to the question 'What justification have we for asserting them?'

Generalisation-laws

Let us first consider 'generalisation-laws', and, as an example, the proposition, 'With a barometric pressure of 30 inches, water boils at 212° Fahrenheit'. Are we justified in asserting categorically such a general proposition as this and, if so, in what does our justification consist? It has sometimes been argued that this, which is not a self-guaranteeing truth of logic, could only be justifiably asserted after repeated experiments, that, if it is to be established at all, it must be established by induction by simple enumeration. But let us imagine that we had satisfactory grounds for asserting that the sample with which we were experimenting was pure water (i.e. that it satisfied the definition or formula for water), and that the conditions under which we were experimenting were both completely controlled and exactly reproducible. Thus we should know that we could repeat the experiment without there being any danger that the conditions, ingredients or equipment would be in any material respect different. Should we, in these circumstances, having once carried through the experiment of measuring the temperature of the water at boiling point, consider that we should repeat the experiment again and again before asserting the result of our experiment universally? Clearly the answer is 'no'. We should say, not merely that it was unnecessary to repeat the experiment, but that to do so would be absurd. This is not to deny that the repetition of experiments is often necessary in order to check the accuracy of earlier experiments ("Did I take the thermometer reading correctly?") or (where we *vary* the conditions of the experiment) in order to establish which factors in the experimental situation were, and which were not, causally relevant to the result.

But are we justified in assuming without question that it would be unnecessary (and absurd) to repeat the same experiment? Let us answer this by considering what would be the consequences if we were to say that we were not so justified. In that case we could *not* take it for granted (as we do) that if identical conditions were reproduced the same result would follow. But if we did not take that for granted we could not significantly experiment at all. For let us assume that the result of experiment 1. was that the liquid boiled at 212° and that the result of experiment 2. was that the liquid boiled at 200°. If we can take it for granted that provided that identical conditions are reproduced identical results follow—let us call this the principle 'same cause, same effect'—then we can know that the difference in the result proves that there was a difference in the conditions. If, however, we cannot assume 'same cause, same effect', we can never decide 1. whether (although, in this case, the 'same cause' *would* have had the 'same effect' had the conditions been exactly reproduced) the conditions were in fact different *or* 2. whether the conditions were exactly reproduced, but, on this occasion, the 'same cause' did *not* have the 'same effect'.

When we assert the general propositions of science it seems that we take for granted two principles, the second of which is really part of the first, namely the principles usually expressed as 'Every event has a cause' and 'same cause, same effect'.

To subscribe to the first principle is not to be committed to the view that scientific laws are of the form 'such-and-such causes such-and-such' but to think of the physical constituents of the world as essentially interacting with one another. The relation of interaction may usefully be described as 'internal' to its related objects, whereas we can describe the spatial relations of objects as 'external' to them. Whether my penknife is in my pocket or on the table in front of me does not affect the nature of my knife. Its spatial relations can change without itself changing. But, just as if Tom is six feet and John five feet tall, Tom cannot but be taller than John because of the height of each, so, analogously, things stand in causal relations to one another because of the properties that they severally possess. For a knife to be sharp is for it to possess a property relevant to its capacity to interact with other things: it can cut wood because it is sharp. We think of physical things as in themselves causally efficacious and capable of interacting with one another. As Locke said, "Powers (are) a great part of our complex ideas of substances". But, further, if the causal relations in which a body A stands to another body B are 'internally related' to the properties that it in itself possesses, then any body possessing those same qualities must interact with other bodies, qualitatively identical with B, in the same way. To recognise the principle 'same cause, same effect' is to recognise what is meant by 'cause' and to grasp one element of the meaning of the sentence "Every event has a cause".

As we have already seen, to adopt an attitude of scepticism to the principle 'same cause, same effect', would be to commit oneself to the admission that all experiment and all attempts to frame general propositions about the world are futile. And this may lead one to suspect that the principle is adopted simply as an expedient in order to make science possible and not as being acceptable in itself. But, it seems to me that we no more choose to adopt the principle than we choose to see the world as consisting of causally interacting things. If we are inclined to doubt this, we should ask ourselves if, for example, we could conceive of a piece of lead which on one occasion sank in water and on another occasion floated, although it underwent no change in itself and although the liquid had the same chemical analysis as the original sample of water.

The physical world is conceived by us as a world of causal interaction. That this is so is neither discovered empirically nor prescribed by ourselves as an expedient devised to make science respectable. But, although it seems that we cannot but think of the world as one in which the principle 'same cause, same effect' holds, we are not similarly bound to think that the same causes should in fact recur, or that there should be in the world numerically different things possessing identical attributes. It is experience that teaches us that things are sufficiently similar for it to be possible for us without artificiality to distinguish things into natural kinds. When philosophers have said that scientific investigation is only possible if nature is uniform, they have sometimes failed to make it clear that the second requirement—that there are things in the world with the same attributes—is not a pre-empirical requirement of science. The principle of causality may intelligibly be called a presupposition of induction. The *observable* uniformity of nature is not; though no doubt a world the constituents of which did not group themselves into kinds would be one about which general propositions could hardly be made.

Before we consider the explanatory hypotheses of science it would be well to explain why this brief but controversial discussion of causality was necessary.

The principle, 'Every event has a cause', with its corollary, 'same cause, same effect', underlies not only the propositions of science but also the general propositions of ordinary discourse. Had that not been so, it might have been possible to omit the discussion of scientific generalisation-laws. But such generalisations of ordinary life as 'Toadstools are poisonous' or 'Trains tend to be delayed by fog' are to be justified, if at all, in the same way as 'Water boils at 212° Fahrenheit'. If it were ever a true and a *complete* account of a situation to say that a given healthy person was made ill by eating toadstools of a certain kind, we should be as much justified in stating generally that toadstools of that particular sort make healthy people ill as we should be in saying, after a single perfectly controlled experiment, that water boils at 212° Fahrenheit. Of course we are more likely to be wrong in the first case than in the second. The conditions under which a man is poisoned by toadstools are more complex, and less easy to establish with certainty, than those in which some controlled laboratory experiments are carried out. This makes it easier for us to misdescribe the original case; perhaps the patient had a particular allergy to fungi, perhaps it was relevant that the fungi were a day old or had been kept in a dirty container, and so on. But if the original case was correctly and completely reported, the universalisation of it involves no unjustified 'leap' from particular to general. Thus a cautious man will be unwilling to generalise from 'The toadstools made George ill' to 'Toadstools make healthy people ill', because, without a greater knowledge of the circumstances than he may possess, he lacks confidence that the original statement, though satisfactory in a rough-and-ready way for ordinary purposes, is complete and accurate. Of course it is not claimed that we can always justifiably pass from propositions about individuals to propositions about totalities. That some professors are absent-minded could never be all that we should need to know to assert that all are. But, if the principle of causality holds, and if it is true that at a barometric pressure of 30 inches a sample of water boils at 212° Fahrenheit, it is logically necessary that at the same barometric pressure any other sample of water would boil at the same temperature.

Explanatory hypotheses

So long as we think of the scientist as propounding generalisations only, it is natural that we should ask what justification he has for asserting his conclusions. But the question ceases to be appropriate if the scientific propositions which he expresses are explanatory hypotheses. If a doctor sees that his patient has a high temperature, he may wonder whether, or guess that, he is suffering from a throat-infection. He needs to provide no justification for making such a hypothesis. We can be sensibly asked to justify our claims only when we go beyond surmise and assert that the explanations which we have suggested are true. It makes no sense to ask what logical right Sir Ronald Ross and his Italian predecessors had to *suggest* that malaria is transmitted by anopheles mosquitoes. That demand comes at a later stage when the scientist not only commits himself to the hypothesis but also asserts that it is a law.

Let us consider what answer would then satisfy us. First, we should need to be shown that if the hypothesis *were* correct, its consequences would be exactly what is observed to be the case: in the example quoted, that every malaria patient examined proved to have been bitten by an anopheles mosquito. Secondly, we should consider the theory strengthened by a controlled experiment; if, for example, anopheles mosquitoes that had bitten malaria patients were then caused to bite healthy subjects who had not been open to other possible sources of infection (where by 'possible sources' is intended what are held to be sources of infection on other theories of the transmission of the disease) and if the previously healthy subjects contracted the disease. If the original hypothesis were that anopheles mosquitoes alone transmitted the disease, further tests would be necessary to falsify the theory that there were also other sources of infection.

It is clear that scientific hypotheses are susceptible of direct confirmation in varying degrees. Thus it may be possible to verify by direct observation that the malaria organism entered the bloodstream of a patient through the bite of a mosquito. Similarly, a detective's theory that a particular suspect was a thief might be directly confirmed if an eye-witness were found or the suspect confessed. On the other hand, however detailed our investigations may be, such physical theories as the Law of Gravitation and the Law of Inertia seem always to escape direct confirmation. There is no point at which the physicist is entitled to say "Now we can see that this body attracts that body in the ratio prescribed in the Law of Gravitation". There remains a gap between theory and observation. Moreover, no general scientific theory can ever be *proved*. If *P* is a given hypothesis, and *Q* the consequences that would occur if the theory were true, the scientist may be entitled to assert 'If *P*, *Q*' and also '*Q*'. But this, of course, does not entitle him to infer the truth of *P*. This would only be possible if he were in a position to assert 'If and only if *P*, *Q*'; and this is the proposition to be proved. However thoroughly he seeks to eliminate all the other conflicting hypotheses that might be put forward to explain the same facts, there is no way of guaranteeing that he will think of and entirely exhaust all the possibilities.

We have not, however, listed all the ways in which a theory is strengthened. Perhaps particularly when theories cannot easily be confirmed by controlled experiments, a scientist may strengthen his case by showing that his theory is of a similar pattern to other theories about kindred subject-matter which have independently been considered acceptable. Thus the theory that yellow fever is transmitted through an insect bite would generally be found more acceptable after it had been agreed that malaria was similarly transmitted. More generally we can say that the simpler a theory is, and the more neatly it can be shown to fall into place in a unified system of theory covering a wide range of phenomena, the more acceptable it is.

Scientific enquiry starts from the assumption that the universe is ordered, for to ask for the explanation of phenomena is to ask for the law which they exemplify. We do not discover that the universe is intelligible, in the sense that it operates in accordance with laws, but, assuming that it is, we try to discover what those laws are. We make an analogous assumption whenever we ask for explanations—for John's bad temper, for the flash on the horizon, for the sense of a difficult passage in a Latin author; for we assume that something or somebody made John angry, that the flash was caused, that the words are not a haphazard jumble of letters but that they were intended by the writer to express a meaning. Since, then, things and events are intelligible in so far as they can be brought under law, it is not surprising that our readiness to accept a proposition as true is direclty proportional to the extent to which it seems to us intelligible. By conceiving the hypothesis of gravitation, Newton showed the movements of the sun and the planets as explicable within one system of law. In showing us that it was intelligible that the sun should rise tomorrow (or any other day) he gave a *good reason* for predicting that it would. Thus, so long as we ask for explanations of phenomena, we are committed to regarding the world as an ordered system and to accepting as reasonable those predictions which accord with the unfalsified principles of order with which observed phenomena are compatible. The hypothetical ordered system may be mistaken, as was, for example, the Ptolemaic system of astronomy. Yet before observations had been made that falsified it, it would have been unreasonable and unjustifiable to make astronomical predictions that were not consistent with its acceptance, except in accordance with some other equally embracing theory, which was consistent both internally and with the observed facts.

When we compare the procedure and methods of scientific investigation with deductive formal logic, we may well feel dissatisfied at the comparative vagueness of the criteria by which we judge the acceptability of the hypotheses and general propositions of science and the reasonableness of scientific predictions. We can check claims that a given argument is deductively valid by truth-tables, by the rules of syllogism or by other strict testing methods which logicians have devised. We can prove it to be true or false. But the only logical relation in which a satisfactory hypothesis stands to the facts which it purports to explain is that of bare compatibility. And though deductive tests for compatibility have been devised, their function is negative. At best we can show that the hypothesis to be tested *may* be true (i.e. that it is consistent with the observed facts). What is lacking is a proof that a given general hypothesis *is* true. In fact, when we are faced with two hypotheses both of which are consistent, have the same scope, and are compatible with all the known facts, there are no rules to which we can appeal for deciding between them or for remaining sceptical and rejecting both. It is true that we consistently prefer the simpler to the more complex theory, provided that the other conditions are satisfied, but in the end our preference seems to be determined by a 'hunch' that one hypothesis 'feels' right and the other wrong.

Scientists sometimes use the word 'elegant' to characterise good hypotheses, but this requirement cannot be expressed in unambiguous concrete terms.

The brief account that I have given of scientific procedure and the scientist's justification in claiming truth for his hypotheses is controversial and one-sided, and the contention that the order of nature which is presupposed by scientific enquiry is causal would be contested, as naive and outdated, by many scientists and philosophers. I have said nothing of 'instrumentalism'; that is to say, the view that scientific hypotheses are to be thought of, not as true or false, but as more or less convenient conceptual frameworks within which the facts under investigation may be regarded. It is clear, too, that there has been over-simplification. Further, the distinction which I have drawn between 'generalisation-laws' and 'explanation-laws' is a layman's, and not a scientist's, distinction and it would be well to remind ourselves of their common features as well as their differences.

It should be recognised that insight is revealed in the scientist's seemingly concrete general propositions as it is in his more obviously explanatory hypotheses. When we try to put together the pieces of a jigsaw-puzzle we sometimes suddenly 'see' a particular piece in a new light. Perhaps we have been looking at it upside-down or have wrongly identified it as part of the sky instead of part of the sea. Suddenly it falls into place. The facts which the scientist sets out to explain are in one respect like the pieces of the jigsaw-puzzle. In translating the elusive 'given' events, objects, processes into propositions, that is to say in describing and reporting them, he interprets them within the conceptual framework of a system. The language in which he reports is a 'theory-laden' language in which descriptions are at the same time interpretations. To speak of a 'nearly hemispherical hollow object made of fibre and metal' would in some contexts be less illuminating and less relevant to our interests than to call it a crash-helmet. If, instead of saying "An apple falls to the ground", one were to say "An unsupported body heavier than air falls to the ground", one would report on the same circumstance in a different light and one that is illuminating in the context of physical theory. It is this characteristic of being systematically illuminating which all the propositions of science have in common and which distinguishes them from the generalisations of everyday life. A good scientific general proposition, whether explanatory or descriptive, is framed in language that is scientifically significant and is fruitful in suggesting methods or lines of investigation.

The work of the scientist does not begin and end with the formulation of explanatory hypotheses and other systematically enlightening general propositions. Most of his time is, no doubt, devoted to the interpretation and working out of problems in the light of the ones already propounded, in devising and operating experimental techniques, in collecting and organising new empirical material, in applying the conclusions of pure science to practical problems. But if we leave aside the part played by imaginative and creative guesswork, these operations seem to involve no other types of reasoning than those with which mathematics and formal logic have made us familiar. To apply theories to particular cases and to establish the interrelatedness of theories within a single system are operations that demand strict logical rigour. In fact the function of a good scientific theory is to represent the problems investigated in such a form that they are capable of being dealt with as problems in mathematics or formal logic. Thus, J. W. L. Glaisher, speaking of Newton's hypothesis that a sphere of gravitating matter attracts bodies outside it as though all its mass were concentrated at the centre, says "No sooner had Newton proved this superb theorem . . . than all the mechanism of the universe lay spread before him . . . It was now in his power to apply mathematical analysis with absolute precision to the actual problems of astronomy."[1] It is not contended, however, that, after formulating his hypothesis, the scientist switches to reasoning purely deductively. Imaginative and creative guesswork, which is essentially what inductive thinking is, is demanded at every stage in the investigations of science and all other disciplines. Often the same speculative originality is required if the scientist is to hit on a way of testing a theory as is required for formulating it in the first place.

Inductive thinking is not a prerogative of the scientist. We think inductively whenever we try to explain. And since to look for an

---

[1] Quoted by W. C. Dampier, *History of Science*, 10th ed., p. 153. It will be noticed that this passage also illustrates the point discussed in the last paragraph.

explanation is to presume that an explanation can in principle be given, we presuppose, when we do so, that what is investigated belongs to an intelligible order. This order need not be causal. If a suspect answers a policeman's questions evasively and the policeman surmises that the man was waiting for a suitable opportunity to break into a jeweller's shop, he is thinking inductively and the order that is presupposed by his hypothesis is purposive. That is to say, the policeman takes it for granted that the man had some *reason* for answering evasively and speculates about what that reason may be. Again, if a student is called on to deduce a logical law from given axioms, he thinks inductively when he tries to reconstruct the intervening valid steps by which he can pass from the axioms to the required conclusion. Here the order presupposed is logical.

The language of induction

Perhaps what has contributed most towards obscuring the difference between deductive and inductive thinking is, to borrow a phrase of Professor Gilbert Ryle, the 'systematic ambiguity' of the vocabulary of induction. The vocabulary of deduction was early absorbed into ordinary language. The use of such words as 'premiss', 'inference', 'conclusion' carries with it no presumption that the user is a student of formal logic. But we have no separate vocabulary in which to express the analysis of inductive thinking. To make good this deficiency philosophers, consciously or unconsciously, took the obvious course and borrowed the language of deduction to do double duty. When we argue deductively we infer from premisses to conclusions. Similarly when we 'induce', we move from observed facts to theories or general propositions. How is this move to be named? Nothing is more natural than that, for want of another word, we should use the word 'infer'. In fact the word 'infer' is more often used in common speech to denote an inductive than a deductive move. But since the same word has two functions it is also natural that we should come to think that the functions themselves are, if not the same, at least very similar. So we are inclined to say that, whereas in a deductive argument the premisses entail the conclusion, in an inductive argument the premisses support or provide good grounds for or probabilify a conclusion.

Here we see how, just as in deductive logic there corresponds to valid inference (i.e. a mental event) the objective logical relationship of entailment holding between premises and conclusions, so it is assumed that a parallel objective inductive logical relationship (that of 'supporting' or 'probabilifying') holds between the 'premisses' and 'conclusion' of legitimate induction. Almost the only words that do not have a dual task are 'valid' and 'entail'. Even the word 'deduction' is used to denote the characteristic act of induction—the formulation of hypotheses. That is its sense in *The Greek Interpreter* when Sherlock Holmes is heard to say of his brother, Mycroft, "I said that he was my superior in observation and deduction". What Conan Doyle meant by 'deduction' here was the gift of making explanatory guesses or theorising. In fact the word 'deduce' is one which many of us probably first met in old-fashioned detective stories.

The ill-effect of this extension in the use of the vocabulary of formal logic has been to lead us to assume that there are two kinds of inference, two kinds of premiss, two kinds of conclusion, two kinds of reasoning or argument—the inductive and the deductive. But there are not; there are two *senses* of 'infer', two senses of 'premiss', two senses of 'conclusion', but there is only one kind of reasoning or argument, namely deductive. If Jones comes into my room dripping with water, I might say "I infer that you were caught in the rain", and the obviousness of the suggestion may mislead one into thinking that it, in a loose sense, *follows from* the fact (or true proposition) that he was wet through. But the fact that Jones was wet not only does not *entail* a conclusion, it does not 'lead' in any direction at all; it is simply a fact to be explained. It may 'provoke' me to ask the question "Why is Jones wet through?", but it does not in any way suggest an answer. The (inductive) 'conclusion' is the hypothesis which *I* (not it) suggest. Even if we were to allow that the bare fact of the repetition of similar occurrences were enough to provoke me to generalise, the repeated occurrences cannot be described otherwise than misleadingly as 'premisses'. At the most they are the occasion of my seeing the possibility that the occurrences may be indefinitely continued. The sequence of thought is essentially similar to that of a great scientist who is set off by a single significant observation to formulate an illuminating theory. It is not difficult to see why the view that there are inductive arguments and inductive reasoning is mistaken. The formulation of a theory does not proceed by steps at all but by flashes of insight (or pseudo-insight). Reasoning is calculation and we do not calculate when we make guesses. Argument comes later when we try to establish that our guesses are compatible with the agreed facts and so on. But this is deductive.

If logic is not the study of thinking but, as I have assumed, the formal study of the relations of logical necessity which may hold between that which is thought—facts and propositions—the study of the formulation of general propositions and hypotheses, of inference in the inductive sense of that word, is not strictly a part of logic. Such thinking conforms to no rules. The creative originality that is displayed by a scientist when he sees phenomena in a new light does not follow paths of reasoning laid down for him. There is no *method* of discovery for logicians to expound.

A SHORT BIBLIOGRAPHY

General works

R. M. Eaton, *General Logic*, New York 1961.
H. W. B. Joseph, *Introduction to Logic*, 2nd ed., Oxford 1916.
P. F. Strawson, *Introduction to Logical Theory*, London 1952.

The first book is one of the best general works on logic, traditional and modern. The second is a useful source-book for traditional logic and the history of theories of induction. The third is a closely-argued account of logical theory from the point of view of modern empiricism and the philosophy of ordinary language.

Other works

B. Russell, *Introduction to Mathematical Philosophy*, London 1919.
G. Frege, *Philosophical Writings of Gottlob Frege* (tr. Geach and Black), Oxford 1952.
—— *The Thought, a logical enquiry* (tr. Quinton), *Mind* 1956.
J. Łukasiewicz, *Aristotle's Syllogistic*, Oxford 1951.
W. V. Quine, *Methods of Logic*, London 1952.
A. N. Prior, *Formal Logic*, Oxford 1955.

In the works of Russell and Frege are to be found some of the most formative ideas and theories in the development of logic. Łukasiewicz re-presents the logic of Aristotle's *Prior Analytics* from the standpoint of modern logic. Quine gives a lively and original presentation of modern formal logic. Prior's book is a scholarly survey of logical systems.

Induction and scientific method

W. C. Kneale, *Probability and Induction*, Oxford 1949.
K. R. Popper, *The Logic of Scientific Discovery*, London 1956.
Stephen Toulmin, *The Philosophy of Science*, London 1953.

Two further books may be mentioned: A. Basson and D. J. O'Connor, *Introduction to Symbolic Logic*, 3rd ed., London 1959; John Passmore, *A Hundred Years of Philosophy*, London 1959.

INDEX

alternative logics, 153
analytic and synthetic, 159–64
Aristotle, 20, 24–5, 32, 36–42, 45–6, 67–8, 70, 73, 145–6
attributes and things, 140–3
Ayer, A. J., 161

categories, 145–9
causality, 178–80
class-membership, 88 ff.
coincidences, 171
conditioned expectations and rational beliefs, 173–4
constants, logical, 49, 137–8
—interpretation of, 59–68
contradiction, 14, 155–9
contraposition, 34
contraries, 32, 157
conventionalism, logical,
    see linguistic-conventionalism
conversion, 33 ff., 44–5
—simple, 34
—*per accidens*, 34
copula, 24
Correspondence Theory of truth, 113–5

'deduction' (inductive), 187
Descriptions, Theory of, 77, 83–7
dictum de omni et nullo, 41–2

Eaton, R. M., 39, 48, 70
empirical verification 112–3
equivalence, material, 49
Euclidean geometry, 40, 57
Ewing, A. C., 161
existence and predication, 75

existential propositions, 74 ff.
explanation, scientific, 174–7, 180–3
—and generalisations, 176
extension, 27, 159

facts, 109–19, 145
—and events, 110–2, 145
fiction, 78–80
form, logical, 12 ff., 118–9
—and validity, 16 ff., 152–3
formal (primitive) concepts, 136–9, 148–9, 151, 153, 165–6
Frege, G., 77, 105, 107

Glaisher, J. W. L., 185

Hume, D., 175
hypothetical propositions, 61–8
—contrary-to-fact, 65–7
—'open', 82

identity propositions,
    see propositions
implication (entailment), 11–12
—material, 49–52, 61–8
induction, 167 ff.
—by simple enumeration, 167, 170–3
—language of, 186–8
inference (deductive), 11, 58–9
    — immediate and mediate, 25, 32–6
    — rules of, 40, 56, 58–9
    — (inductive), 186–8
intension, 159
inversion, 35

190

Kant, I., 73, 145, 159–61
knowledge, theory of, 112

'laws of thought', 19, 57, 69–70
linguistic-conventionalism,
        120 ff., 133–5, 147–8
—and formal logic, 126–33
—and 'non-formal logic', 122–6
Locke, J., 144, 178
logic, 9 ff.
—and language
    see linguistic conventionalism
—and psychology, 11, 60, 107
—formal and non-formal, 18,
        121–6
—of propositions, 19, 48, ch. 3,
        165
    see also propositional calculus
—of terms, 19–20, ch. 2, 94–5
    see also predicative calculus
—traditional (of terms), ch. 2
— —as a system, 40–1
— —criticisms of, 35, 42–6
logical impossibilities, 68–70
logical necessity, 9 ff., 154–5,
        164–6
—and analyticity, 159–64
—and self-contradiction, 155–9
Łukasiewicz, J., 21 *footnote*, 42,
        45–6, 67–8

material equivalence,
    see equivalence
material implication,
    see implication
meaning, 22, 102–5, 117, 154–5
Meinong, A., 79
Mill, J. S., 175
modus ponens and *modus tollens*,
        47

necessary and contingent, 10
negation 130–3, 136–7

Newton, I., 176, 183

obversion, 34

Pap, A., 161
Peano, G., 77
predicative calculus, 75, 94–9
presuppositions, 35, 45, 74, 76,
        80–2
Principia Mathematica, 40, 55,
        94, 96–7, 137–8
proper names, 75–6, 78–80, 89
propositional calculus, 49 ff.
—and ordinary language, 70–2
propositional functions, 77, 80–3
propositional variables, 19, 49
propositions, 13–14, 101–5, ch. 5
—and facts, 109–15
—and sentences, 13–14, 20, 101–
        105, 123
—and statements, 105–9
—existential, 74 ff.
—general, 24, 76–7
—hypothetical,
    see hypothetical propositions
—identification of, 115–9
—of identity, 87–94
—particular, 24, 82–3
—subject-predicate,
    see subject-predicate
—universal, 24, 44–5, 80–2

quality, 25
quantification, quantifiers, 54,
        87, 95
quantity, 25
Quine, W. V., 66

referring expressions, 74, 76–83,
        91
relations, logic of, 23, 146–7,
        149–53

rules and principles, 57–9, 71, 153

Russell, B., 40, 55, 70, 76–9, 80, 83–4, 94–5

Ryle, G., 186

'same cause, same effect', 177–80

Schlick, M., 160

scope, 50 *footnote*

sentences,
 see propositions

square of opposition, 32, 44–5

statements,
 see propositions

Stebbing, L. S., 29 *footnote*

Stoics, 42, 48

Strawson, P. F., 71, 86, 98–9, 107, 120, 122, 127–31, 133, 152, 156, 161–2

stroke-function, 49, 137–8

subject and predicate, 15, 24 ff., 73–7, 78–81, 139–40

substitution
—by definition, 56
—on variables, 56

syllogism, 21, 25 ff.
—figures of, 26
—mood-names of, 31–2
—moods of, 26
—perfect and imperfect, 36
—reduction of
— —direct, 36–8
— —indirect, 38–40
—rules of, 28–32

term-variables, 15, 19

terms, 24–6
—distribution of, 27 ff.
—non-empty, 45

things and attributes, 140–3

'truth by definition', 162–3

truth-functional analysis, 56, 63–4

truth, logical,
 see logical necessity

truth-tables, 52–4

Waismann, F., 160, 163

Whitehead, A. N., 40, 55, 94